They Shall Be One
A Blueprint for Marital Harmony and Healing

By
Christopher K. Turney

MARRIAGE SERIES
KRMI (Kingdom Reign Marriage Institute)

They Shall Be One
A Blueprint for Marital Harmony and Healing
Copyright © 2025 by Christopher K. Turney
All rights reserved.

No part of this book may be reproduced, stored in a retrieval system, or transmitted in any form or by any means, electronic, mechanical, photocopy, recording, or otherwise, without prior written permission from the publisher, except for brief quotations in reviews.

Scripture quotations, unless otherwise noted, are taken from the Holy Bible.

ISBN: 979-8-9943976-0-2
Printed in the United States of America.

DEDICATION

To every husband and wife who believed love was lost when in truth it was only buried beneath pain, fear, and misunderstanding.

To those who stayed.
To those who left but still ache.
To those who want to believe again but need truth to heal first.

And to those who will build a marriage that speaks redemption louder than failure ever could.

ACKNOWLEDGEMENTS

This book exists because of every couple who trusted me with their story. Every tear shed across a table, every confession whispered through shame, every moment of anger, betrayal, heartbreak, and hope shaped the revelation in these pages.

To my spiritual father and mother who modeled covenant, correction, and endurance, thank you for showing me that love is not sustained by emotion alone, but by divine order and holy commitment.

To the sons and daughters who allowed me to walk with them through the fire of restoration, this book carries your victory.

And above all, to the Lord Jesus Christ, who came to a broken Bride, refused to abandon her in her worst condition, and paid the ultimate price to present her whole. This mystery is the foundation of every truth written here.

CONTENTS

Preface 1
Introduction 5
  1. Before There Was a Wedding, There Was a Design 11
  2. They Shall Be One: The Mystery of Covenant Union 19
  3. Ezer: The Power of Divine Partnership 27
  4. Submission, Safety, and Abuse: Restoring What Fear Has Distorted 35
  5. When Two Purposeful People Never Define One Shared Mission 43
  6. Calling Without Confusion: Her Mission & His Headship in God's Design 53
  7. The Clashing of Normals: When Two Histories Collide in Covenant 69
  8. When Your Spouse Stops Being a Safe Place 75
  9. Money Problems or Partnering Problems? 83
  10. When Differences Become "Irreconcilable" 91
  11. Love, Choice, and the Myth of "Falling Out" 99
  12. Romance, Covenant, and the War Between Feeling and Faithfulness 107
  13. Did God Ever Enter the Marriage? Returning to the Beginning for Healing 115
  14. Compatible Purpose or Convenient Choice? 123
  15. Loving Who They Will Become, Not Just Who They Are 129
  16. When Submission Becomes a Threat Instead of a Trust ... 137
  17. The War Between Appreciation and Resentment 145

18. When Money Becomes the Enemy Instead of the Assignment 153
19. From Lovers to Strangers: How Friendship Dies in Marriage, and How It Can Live Again 159
20. What Men Need to Know About Women 165
21. What Women Need to Know About Men 173
22. A New Beginning: A Step-by-Step Path to Healing and Harmony 179

Conclusion 191
A Final Word to Husbands and Wives 193
A Prayer for Couples 195
For Reflection & Rebuilding 197
About the Author 199

PREFACE
RETURNING TO THE BEGINNING

I have sat across tables from couples who swore they were finished. Some were angry. Some were numb. Some were exhausted. Some still loved each other but no longer recognized each other. Almost every one of them said the same things in different ways. "We have money problems." "We don't communicate." "We grew apart." "We're just different now." "We tried everything." After pastoring, counseling, and walking with married couples for decades, I have discovered a sobering truth: most marriages do not fail because they run out of love, they fail because they lose alignment.

Money was never the real issue. Communication was never the root problem. Busyness was not the true enemy, and personality differences were not the silent killer. What was lost was not affection, but agreement. What fractured was not attraction, but partnership. What eroded was not desire, but shared direction. Two people can love each other deeply and still drift miles apart when they stop walking toward the same purpose. Love can remain sincere while alignment quietly dissolves. And when alignment is gone, every pressure feels heavier, every disagreement feels sharper, and every hardship feels personal.

This is why couples so often fight about money when the real battle is trust. They argue about communication when the deeper wound is safety. They blame growing apart when the truth is they stopped growing together. I have learned that marriage does not usually end in one dramatic moment. It ends in a thousand subtle disconnections, unguarded moments where understanding gave way to assumption, where honor yielded to disappointment, where presence surrendered to distraction, and where partnership was slowly replaced by parallel lives.

And yet, I have also learned something just as powerful: if what was lost was alignment, then what must be restored is alignment. Healing does not begin with fixing behavior. Healing begins with realigning hearts. This is why some couples can survive financial collapse, sickness, betrayal, and unspeakable pressure, while others collapse under everyday life. The difference is not strength, it is shared direction. It is the quiet, daily decision to remain joined in purpose even when emotions fluctuate.

Marriage does not need more survival strategies. It needs restored covenant vision. And that is the space this book was written to serve. Most couples do not actually have the problems they think they have. They believe they have financial problems, but what they really have are partnership problems. They believe they have communication problems, but what they really have are safety problems. They believe they have irreconcilable differences, but what they truly carry are unhealed value fractures and unresolved honor wounds.

And many of them once believed the most dangerous lie of all, that if God brought them together, everything should be easy. It isn't. And it never was designed to be. I know this personally. I have lived inside broken relationships. I have believed in the "the one" myth. I once thought that revelation, prayer, fasting, prophecy, and spiritual language would automatically make love permanent and unity effortless. It did not. Not because God was absent, but because God was never truly invited into the beginning the way He should have been.

Genesis did not begin with a wedding. It began with a design. And healing does not begin with behavior modification. It begins with returning to design. That is what this book exists to do.

This is not a book about staying married at all costs. This is a book about becoming one the right way. It is about becoming safe for each other again. It is about becoming partners instead of opponents, builders instead of blamers, healed instead of hardened.

This book is about marital reconstruction, not just survival.

Many couples are not failing because they are evil. They are failing because they were never taught how to build as one. They were taught how to date, attract, impress, perform, and pursue, but never how to partner, cover, conflict in safety, carry each other's weakness without weaponizing it, or face pressure together instead of turning on each other.

One of the most painful realizations in any struggling marriage is this: your differences did not suddenly appear one day. They were there when you met. They were there when you fell in love. They were there when you stood at the altar. They only became "irreconcilable" when honor disappeared.

When value erodes, grace disappears. When grace disappears, patience dries up. When patience dries up, anger replaces empathy. When empathy dies, partners become enemies.

This book teaches you how to restore honor, rebuild value, recover safety, and return to unity without losing yourself in the process. And it all centers on one question that ultimately determines the future of every marriage: Was God truly invited into this covenant when it began? Not, "Did we pray at the wedding?" Not, "Did a pastor marry us?" Not, "Did we mean well?" But did God author the union, or did we simply ask Him to bless a decision we had already made?

And here is the hope that changes everything: even if God was not invited into the beginning, He can be invited in now. After five years. After twenty years. After fifty years. Alignment is never locked out by time. You can repent, not in shame, but in realignment. The Greek word metanoeo does not mean regret; it means to change the way you think. It means to shift perspective, to rebuild from truth, to realign with original design, and to return to the beginning and start again, this time with God at the center.

This book is not a lecture. It is not a manifesto. It is not a list of demands. It is a healing table, a rebuilding blueprint, a restoration manual, and a return-to-one invitation. If your marriage is strong, this book will help protect it. If your marriage is wounded, it will help heal it. If your marriage is cold, it will help rekindle it. And if your marriage is fragile, it will help strengthen the cord of three that cannot be broken.

And if you are willing to begin again…

They shall be one.

INTRODUCTION
FROM A WEDDING TO A WAY OF LIFE

The Most Celebrated Day, and the Most Neglected Blueprint

For many couples, the moment of engagement launches one of the most intense seasons of planning they will ever experience. Time, money, emotional energy, and stress are poured into a single event called a wedding. Months, sometimes years, are consumed with decisions about venues, colors, clothing, music, seating charts, flowers, photography, food, and guest lists. Every detail is scrutinized. Every opinion is weighed. Every dollar is stretched. In some cases, couples even begin their life together in debt, just to ensure the day is unforgettable.

What is tragic is not that a wedding is celebrated. Celebration is good. What is tragic is that the celebration is often given more attention than the covenant it is meant to introduce. The originating event becomes the focus, while the lifelong construction is left undefined. The wedding becomes the goal, instead of the doorway.

In other cases, the opposite happens. There is no grand event at all. A quiet courthouse ceremony, minimal witnesses, little preparation. Sometimes this simplicity reflects wisdom and restraint. But other times it reflects something else, an unspoken awareness that something significant is missing, unnamed, unresolved, or unprepared. Whether extravagant or minimal, both extremes often share the same blind spot: the marriage itself is rarely the true focus.

The irony is this: we plan intensely for a day, but not always for a lifetime.

When Events Replace Enjoyment

This imbalance is not accidental. It is the product of a culture that conditions us to believe that enjoyment must always be attached to something eventful. We are trained to think connection requires a vacation, a holiday, a family gathering, a celebration, or a special experience. In subtle ways, we are discipled into believing that the event is what gives us pleasure.

But marriage was never meant to work that way.

In covenant, the joy was never supposed to come primarily from the event, it was supposed to come from each other. The shared life was meant to be the reward. The partnership was meant to be the pleasure. The intimacy was meant to be the refuge.

When couples unconsciously adopt the belief that joy must always be externally manufactured, something dangerous happens. Ordinary life begins to feel empty. Daily partnership begins to feel mundane. The shared mission begins to feel burdensome. Instead of drawing fulfillment from one another, they begin to wait for the next event to feel alive again.

This creates a subtle but damaging precedent at the very beginning of the marriage: We enjoy each other best when something special is happening, instead of because something sacred has happened.

There is a dangerous confusion in our culture between a wedding and a marriage. A wedding is an event, but a marriage is a construction. A wedding happens in a moment, but a marriage unfolds across a lifetime. A wedding is a declaration, but a marriage is a daily demonstration. A wedding can be breathtakingly beautiful and still be hollow, while a marriage can be deeply difficult and still be profoundly right.

Our culture trains us to invest extraordinary time, money, emotion, and energy into a single day, while often giving little thought to the decades that are meant to follow it. The result is that many couples begin their lives together celebrating something they have not yet learned how to build. They plan for the ceremony, but not for the covenant. They prepare for the photographs, but not for the process. And so they enter marriage with expectations formed by an event, rather than by a design.

This is why so many couples feel disoriented once the wedding passes. The music fades, the guests leave, the decorations come down, and real life begins. When the marriage was built on the momentum of a moment rather than the foundation of a mission, disappointment is almost inevitable. But when the marriage is anchored in covenant vision rather than ceremonial excitement, even the hardest seasons can still be held together by purpose.

When couples confuse these two, they often begin their covenant with emotional momentum but without spiritual architecture. They celebrate loudly what they have not yet learned how to steward. They announce publicly what they have not yet learned how to build privately.

And then, when the stress of life settles in, finances, exhaustion, children, conflict, unfulfilled expectations, they are shocked to discover that celebration cannot sustain what construction was never taught to support.

This is not because they are wicked. It is because they were never given a blueprint.

This book does not exist to critique weddings. It exists to restore marriage to its original design. It exists because too many couples entered covenant sincerely, spiritually, and passionately, yet without a clear understanding of why they were truly joined, what they were meant to build, how they were designed to function together, what partnership requires, and what God intended marriage to display in the earth. Many couples did not fail morally; they failed architecturally. They were given vows, but not a vision. They were given roles, but not revelation. They were given ceremony, but not construction.

This is the journey from romance to representation. From emotional connection to covenant demonstration. From the excitement of falling in love to the holy work of becoming one. Marriage was never meant to be merely a private relationship between two people; it was always designed to be a public testimony of Christ and His Church, a living image of divine partnership displayed in the earth. This book exists to help guide that transition, to move couples out of survival mode and into covenant purpose, out of confusion and into clarity, out of coexistence and into construction.

At its highest level, marriage is not merely romantic, it is representational. It was designed to point to something far greater than emotional fulfillment. It was meant to reveal Christ and His Church. It was meant to display covenant love, sacrificial leadership, faithful partnership, redemptive endurance, and generational purpose.

This is why marriage carries so much personal pressure and spiritual weight. When it thrives, it reflects heaven. When it fractures, it wounds deeply, because it was never meant to be casual.

What you are holding is not a book about how to plan better weddings. It is a book about how to recover God's intention for becoming one.

An Invitation to Begin Again, The Right Way

Some who read this will be newly engaged. Others will be newly married. Many will be years, perhaps decades, into covenant. Some will be carrying wounds, disappointments, betrayals, and exhaustion. Some will still be hopeful but confused. Some will be strong but quietly afraid of what could one day unravel.

This book speaks to all of you, no matter where your marriage is right now. It does not begin with shame; it begins with design. It does not begin with blame; it begins with alignment. It does not begin at the altar; it begins in Genesis. Because the only way to truly heal what is broken in the middle is to return to what was spoken in the beginning.

CHAPTER 1
BEFORE THERE WAS A WEDDING, THERE WAS A DESIGN

The First Marriage Was Not a Romance

Marriage did not begin with flowers, vows, music, or a crowd of witnesses. It began in silence, before sin, before shame, before fear, before competition, and before self-protection. The first marriage was formed in the atmosphere of God's original intention. There was no rehearsal dinner. There was no ceremony. There was only design.

This matters, because everything that breaks in marriage later is rooted in what was first misunderstood at the beginning. We do not heal marriage by mastering techniques. We heal marriage by returning to original architecture. Long before there was a wedding, God established a way of life called covenant partnership.

Genesis does not introduce marriage as a social institution. It introduces it as a governmental union. God creates a man, gives him a mandate, and then declares something shocking: "It is not good that the man should be alone." This statement is not emotional, it is functional. God is not saying Adam is lonely. God is saying Adam is insufficient to accomplish the mandate alone.

Adam had access to God.
Adam had dominion.
Adam had authority.
Adam had perfection.

Yet something was still missing. Not affection, capacity.

A Man With a Mission

Before a woman ever entered the picture, a man already had an assignment. God placed Adam in the garden "to tend it and to keep it." This was not gardening. This was government. Adam was given territory to steward, order to maintain, and authority to establish. He was given work before he was given a wife.

This is foundational. A man is not defined first by relationship. He is defined first by responsibility. Relationship does not give a man direction, direction gives relationship meaning.

This is where many modern marriages begin in reverse. We look for companionship before calling. We look for intimacy before instruction. We look for chemistry before commission. But in Genesis, God establishes a mission before He introduces marriage.

Why? Because marriage is designed to serve a purpose greater than itself.

The Woman Was Not Created for Adam's Comfort, But for Adam's Calling

When God creates the woman, He does not say, "I will make him someone to love." He says, "I will make him a helper." The Hebrew word used here is ezer. This word does not mean assistant, servant, or subordinate. It means strong rescuer, essential support, life-supplying counterpart.

It is the very same word Scripture uses to describe God Himself as Israel's helper. This means the woman was never created to be less than the man; she was created to be what the man lacked for the mission. She was not made to follow weakness. She was made to fortify purpose.

The woman does not merely join the man's life. She upgrades his capacity to fulfill his mandate. She does not compete with the mission. She multiplies it. This is why the empowering capacity of a wife is not found in simply being under a man, it is found in being engaged with his God-given assignment.

Until a woman is connected to a mission, her power has no divine target. And when power has no target, it turns inward into frustration, control, exhaustion, or isolation. But when a woman aligns herself with God's purpose in her husband, she enters the highest activation of her calling as a wife.

Not as a woman, but as a wife.

Partnership Was the First Picture of Power

Genesis reveals something extraordinary: God never intended the man to rule alone. Dominion was always meant to be shared. The woman was not created to admire the mission from a distance. She was created to co-labor inside it.

This is why marriage is not two individuals coexisting. It is two partners co-building under God. And this is precisely why the New Testament later reveals marriage as a "great mystery" that represents Christ and the Church. Christ does not merely rule. He invites partnership. The Church does not merely observe. She participates.

Marriage was designed to function the same way.

Covenant Is Not About Feelings, It Is About Assignment

Romance came later. Emotion followed purpose. Affection followed alignment. But the foundation was never feeling, it was function.

This is why modern marriage often collapses under pressure. We were trained to marry for how someone makes us feel, not for what God called us to build together. When feelings shift, and they always do, many believe love has died. But love was never meant to be sustained by feeling alone. It was meant to be sustained by faithful purpose shared in covenant.

This is also why many couples believe they have money problems when they actually have partnering problems. They believe they have communication problems when they actually have safety problems. They believe they have irreconcilable differences when, in truth, honor quietly eroded over time.

None of that is healed by romance. It is healed by rebuilding partnership.

You Did Not Just Marry a Person, You Married a Formation

Before two people ever stand at an altar, they have already been shaped by a household. They bring with them a culture they did not choose, a conflict style they did not consciously design, an emotional reflex they did not intentionally create. They do not marry a family, but they absolutely marry what a family made them to be.

This is why the "clashing of normals" is inevitable.

Two worlds collide. Two definitions of love meet. Two understandings of safety confront one another. Two ways of handling anger, affection, money, authority, silence, and stress are suddenly joined in covenant. Marriage does not erase these differences, it exposes them under pressure.

This is why many couples are stunned after the wedding. They say, "You've changed," when in reality, they are simply meeting the version of their spouse that pressure reveals.

This is not a reason for despair. It is a reason for renegotiation.

Covenant does not trap you in your family's past. Covenant gives you the authority to rewrite normal. The question is not whose way is right. The question is: What culture are we intentionally building now?

Marriage Is Not About Getting Your Dream, It Is About Giving Yourself to Theirs

Marriage is not about meeting the person who will make your dreams come true. It is about meeting the person whose dreams you are willing to help make come true. This is the pattern of Christ and the Church. Christ did not come to fulfill Himself. He came to give Himself.

Paul's words are not romantic exaggeration. They are architectural truth. Marriage reveals something far greater than two people in love, it reveals redemptive purpose.

With compatible purpose, we live in fulfillment.
With selfish ambition, we destroy each other.

When two people chase personal fulfillment, marriage becomes competitive. When two people give themselves to shared purpose, marriage becomes generative.

The First Fracture Was Not Between a Man and a Woman, But Between Purpose and Trust

The fall did not begin as a marital conflict. It began as a governmental rupture. The serpent did not attack Adam and Eve's romance, he attacked their trust in God's word and order. From that moment forward, domination, control, fear, withdrawal, and competition began to invade what was once partnership.

Everything Paul later addresses in Ephesians about love and submission is not oppression, it is **restoration**. Husbands are commanded to return to sacrificial love. Wives are invited to relinquish the impulse to rule. Both are called back to the original order where neither dominated and neither withdrew.

Christ is the pattern.
The Church is the partner.
And marriage becomes the living parable again.

You Are Not Just Married to Who They Are, You Are Married to Who God Is Making Them to Be

One of the great blind spots in marriage is that we covenant with a version of a person, not realizing God is still shaping them. Many spouses pray for change, until that change actually disrupts the power dynamics they learned to live with.

Some wives want leadership until leadership requires submission. Some husbands enjoy dependence until God heals her and she no longer needs him the way she used to. Growth exposes insecurity. Healing threatens control. And transformation often becomes the very thing marriage resists instead of celebrates.

Real covenant does not say, "I love who you are." Real covenant says, "I will honor who God is forming you into, even when it requires me to change too."

Why We Must Return to Design

We cannot fix modern marriage by perfecting cultural models. We must return to Genesis architecture. We must restore mission before romance, covenant before chemistry, purpose before pleasure, and partnership before preference.

Because long before there was a wedding, there was a design. And every lasting marriage is built on the courage to return to it.

CHAPTER 2

THEY SHALL BE ONE: THE MYSTERY OF COVENANT UNION

Marriage as a Mystery, Not a Mechanism

When the apostle Paul speaks about marriage, he does something unexpected. He does not reduce it to compatibility, romance, shared interests, or emotional satisfaction. Instead, he calls it a mystery.

"This is a great mystery," he writes, "but I speak concerning Christ and the Church."

A mystery is not something confusing. A mystery is something revealed only by God. By calling marriage a mystery, Paul is declaring that marriage cannot be fully understood by psychology, culture, or human logic alone. Its deepest meaning is unlocked only when we see it as a divine representation.

Marriage is not merely two people choosing each other. It is two people portraying something eternal.

When a husband and wife stand in covenant, heaven is not merely witnessing a personal commitment. Heaven is witnessing a living parable of Christ and His Bride. This is why marriage carries such spiritual weight. It is not just relational, it is theological. It preaches without words. It demonstrates without sermons. It reveals either redemption or distortion every single day.

This is also why the enemy hates marriage. Not because of romance, not because of companionship, but because marriage proclaims the gospel in visible form. When marriage thrives, Christ is glorified. When marriage fractures, the image of covenant love is wounded.

Covenant Is Not a Contract

One of the greatest errors of modern marriage is that it is often approached like a contract instead of embraced as a covenant. A contract is built on mutual benefit, but a covenant is built on mutual giving. A contract says, "I will, as long as you do," while a covenant says, "I will, even when you don't."

A contract is designed to protect rights, but a covenant is an offering of self. A contract is enforced by law, but a covenant is sealed by surrender. And when marriage is treated like a contract, love becomes conditional, endurance becomes negotiable, and unity becomes fragile. But when marriage is embraced as a covenant, sacrifice becomes holy, faithfulness becomes steadfast, and oneness becomes unbreakable.

This is why so many marriages collapse under pressure. When trial comes, people instinctively retreat into contractual thinking. They begin to measure fairness. They begin to calculate effort. They begin to weigh who is giving more and who is failing most. But covenant was never designed to operate on the scales of fairness. Covenant operates on the altar of self-giving.

Christ did not enter into a contract with the Church. He entered into a covenant. He did not say, "I will love you if you remain perfect." He said, "I will love you while I perfect you."

Marriage was designed to mirror that same posture.

"One" Is Not a Feeling, It Is a Formation

When Scripture declares, "They shall be one," it is not describing romance. It is describing union. One is not a sensation. One is a new reality formed by covenant.

Two minds begin to think with shared perspective.
Two wills begin to move with shared direction.
Two lives begin to submit to shared purpose.

Oneness is not intense chemistry.
Oneness is integrated direction.

This is why marriage cannot survive on feelings alone. Feelings fluctuate. Oneness must be built. It must be cultivated through agreement, sacrifice, communication, repentance, endurance, and common mission. Oneness is not discovered, it is constructed.

And it is always constructed under pressure.

Why Romance Was Never Meant to Be the Foundation

There is nothing wrong with romance. God created attraction. God designed desire. God wired affection. But He never designed romance to be the foundation of marriage. Romance is meant to be the reward, not the root.

When romance is made foundational, marriage becomes fragile. The moment desire cools, affection shifts, or chemistry weakens, the entire structure begins to shake. People conclude they must have married the wrong person because they no longer feel what they once felt.

But covenant never asked permission from feelings.

Marriage was built on assignment, agreement, and self-giving, not on emotional momentum. Romance flourishes best when it rests on the unshakable ground of purpose and covenant. But when romance is treated as the ground itself, it eventually collapses under the weight it was never designed to bear.

The Cost of Loving Who They Will Become

One of the most overlooked realities of covenant is this: you are not just marrying who they are, you are marrying who God is shaping them into.

Transformation is not a threat to marriage, it is the environment marriage was built for. But many couples unknowingly covenant with a version of their spouse that suits their comfort, their control, or their insecurity. And when God begins to heal, mature, deliver, or elevate that spouse, resistance emerges.

Some wives pray for strong leadership until that leadership displaces their control.

Some husbands enjoy dependence until God heals the woman and she no longer needs them the same way.

Healing rearranges power dynamics. Growth exposes insecurity. Maturity disrupts old agreements. And when one spouse grows while the other refuses to adjust, covenant strain begins not because love is absent, but because transformation is being resisted.

True covenant love does not cling to who someone used to be. It embraces who God is forming them to become, even when it requires personal repositioning.

When One Grows and the Other Remains

One of the most painful seasons in any marriage is when spiritual growth becomes asymmetrical. One spouse begins to pursue God with sincerity. Their hunger deepens. Their conviction sharpens. Their alignment strengthens. Meanwhile, the other spouse grows stagnant, resistant, or indifferent.

This creates unique tension. The growing spouse feels alone. The stagnant spouse feels judged. Silence replaces understanding. Distance replaces intimacy.

This is where covenant must rise above comfort.

Marriage does not require both spouses to grow at the same speed, but it does require both spouses to honor growth when it comes. When growth is celebrated, unity deepens. When growth is resented, unity fractures.

The question that determines the future is not, "Are we growing equally?"

It is, "Are we honoring what God is doing in each other without turning it into a rivalry?"

Love Is Not Missing, Choice Is

Many spouses say, "I asked God to give me love for them, and He didn't."

But if God commanded us to love our enemies, then He has already empowered us with the capacity to love our spouse. The issue is not supply. The issue is surrender.

Love is not first a feeling.
Love is first a valuation.

People do not fall out of love. They retreat from value. They pull back honor. They protect themselves from disappointment. They shut down vulnerability. And once value is withdrawn, blame begins to replace responsibility.

Love was not missing.
Choice was.

Covenant love says, "I will continue to value you even when my emotions feel unsettled." This does not excuse sin. It does not tolerate abuse. But it does refuse the lie that love is purely emotional and therefore optional when feelings shift.

The Real Opponent of Covenant: Self-Preservation

The greatest enemy of covenant is not incompatibility. It is self-preservation. The moment survival becomes the highest goal, surrender is no longer possible. People stop asking, "How do we win together?" and begin asking, "How do I protect myself?"

Covenant only works when both people are willing to risk self-interest for shared purpose. The moment marriage becomes two people negotiating safety instead of building together, oneness begins to erode.

Christ did not preserve Himself to save the Church. He gave Himself. And that is the exact posture covenant requires.

From Union to Legacy

Marriage was never meant to terminate in personal happiness alone. It was meant to produce legacy. It was meant to shape future generations. It was meant to create stability where chaos once ruled. It was meant to model God's nature in the earth.

This is why marriage is not casual.
Not temporary.
Not disposable.

It is holy because it represents something holy.

They shall be one, not simply because they feel close, but because they are aligned in covenant, anchored in purpose, and surrendered to a mission greater than themselves.

CHAPTER 3

EZER: THE POWER OF DIVINE PARTNERSHIP

The Word That Changed Everything

Few words in Scripture have been more misunderstood, and more misused, than the word translated helper. When God said, "It is not good that the man should be alone; I will make him a helper," centuries of distorted interpretation reduced that word to something small, subordinate, and secondary.

But the Hebrew word used in Genesis is not a weak word. It is the word **ezer (עֵזֶר)**.

This word does not mean assistant.
It does not mean servant.
It does not mean sidekick.

It means strong rescuer, essential strength, one who supplies what is lacking.

This same word is repeatedly used in the Old Testament to describe God Himself as the helper of Israel. God is called ezer in passages such as Psalm 33:20, Psalm 70:5, and Psalm 121:1–2. In every case, the word describes power, defense, and necessary intervention, not inferiority.

So when God says He created the woman as an ezer for the man, He is not diminishing her, He is revealing her strategic power.

The Empowering Capacity of a Wife

The empowering capacity of a woman is not found in being under a man.

It is found in supporting his mission.
Position alone is not empowerment.
Purpose alignment is.

From the beginning, the woman was not created to orbit the man's personality, comfort his insecurity, or serve his ego. She was created to engage God's assignment in his life. She was formed to support the execution of something larger than emotion, a divine mandate.

This is why a woman's power as a wife is distinct from her power as a woman.

As a woman, she carries inherent strength, intuition, discernment, creativity, nurture, and endurance. But as a wife, that strength becomes mission-activated. She becomes a multiplier of direction, a stabilizer of calling, and a reinforcer of destiny.

When a woman aligns herself with a man's God-identified mission, not his moods, not his fears, not his preferences, she enters the highest activation of her calling as a wife. This is where her potency is maximized, where her influence becomes generational.

Not because she is diminished, but because her power now has a divine target.

Submission Is Not Silence, It Is Undergirding

Submission has been so deeply misrepresented that many recoil from the word instantly. But biblically, submission has nothing to do with inferiority.

To submit means to undergird.

The Greek word Paul uses in Ephesians 5:22 for submit is hypotassō (ὑποτάσσω). It means:
- To arrange oneself under
- To align under order
- To come into proper sequence

It is not forced obedience.
It is willing alignment with divine order.

Submission does not mean disappearance.
It does not mean voicelessness.
It does not mean tolerating abuse.

It means supporting the structure that God has established so that it can rise. It means to come underneath something in order to uphold it.

You place a pillar underneath a structure not because it is weak, but because it is valuable and destined to rise higher.

This is why Scripture does not tell a woman to submit to "men" in general. It tells her to submit to her own husband. This is a specific covenant alignment, not a universal domination structure. A wife is not placed under male authority as a gender category. She is aligned with one man in a God-ordered partnership.

And the reason this alignment works is not because the man is superior, it is because the mission is sacred.

A Man Without a Mission Leaves a Woman Nothing to Support

Here is a truth that must be spoken plainly:
A woman cannot biblically submit to a man who has no mission, because there is nothing to get under.

Submission is not to personality.
It is not to insecurity.
It is not to passivity.
It is not to emotional impulse.

Submission is to purpose under God.

When a man has no assignment, no direction, no God-defined responsibility, the woman is left trying to support motion instead of mandate. And when leadership is absent, frustration is inevitable. Control often fills the vacuum where purpose was never established.

This is why some women become managing, compensating, or dominating, not because they are rebellious, but because they are trying to stabilize what was never structured.

A woman was never designed to submit to aimlessness. She was designed to undergird calling.

Headship: A Threefold Order of Protection

Paul reveals a divine sequence in 1 Corinthians 11:3:
"The head of every man is Christ, the head of woman is man, and the head of Christ is God."

This is not hierarchy for control, it is sequence for covering.

When a man is genuinely under Christ, His authority, His nature, His government, then a woman who aligns with that man is also under Christ. She is not indirectly under God. She is directly covered by Christ through divine order.

But something critical must be understood:
If the man moves out from under Christ, he does not move the woman with him.

A man does not have the authority to reposition a woman out from under Christ. Her allegiance is first to God, not to dysfunction, rebellion, sin, or abuse. If a man abandons Christ's government, the woman must remain aligned with Christ even if it means she is no longer aligned with him.

Biblical submission never binds a woman to terror, violence, or spiritual abandonment. Scripture never commands a woman to undergird sin.

What Actually Broke in Genesis 3

When sin entered the world, it did not only damage humanity's relationship with God. It also restructured the power dynamics between man and woman.

God speaks to the woman after the Fall:
"Your desire shall be for your husband, and he shall rule over you." (Genesis 3:16)

The Hebrew word translated desire here is teshuqah (תְּשׁוּקָה). This same word appears again in Genesis 4:7 when God speaks to Cain:

"Sin's desire (teshuqah) is for you, but you must rule over it."

This shows clearly that teshuqah does not mean affection. It means an impulse to control, master, or dominate.

Genesis 3:16 is not God endorsing domination. It is God describing the tragic distortion sin introduced into marriage: a struggle for control and a collapse of sacrificial love.

Before the Fall → partnership under God
After the Fall → power struggle between man and woman

Adam's Sin Was Abdication, Not Aggression

Genesis 3 reveals that Adam was with Eve at the moment of deception. He did not intervene. He did not confront. He did not protect. He withdrew from leadership.

Later Scripture confirms this:
"Adam was not deceived, but the woman was deceived and became a transgressor." (1 Timothy 2:14)

Adam's failure was not dominance; it was silent abdication. Instead of guarding, he became passive. Instead of leading, he yielded responsibility. Instead of protecting order, he participated in its collapse. And so, after the Fall, a fracture entered the heart of marriage: men drifted from sacrificial leadership into withdrawal, and women drifted from supportive partnership into control. This is the very fracture the apostle Paul is addressing, not by reinforcing distortion, but by restoring order through redemption.

Why Paul Commands Love and Submission Differently

When Paul writes in Ephesians 5, he is not introducing inequality, he is applying spiritual precision to restore Eden's fracture.

"Husbands, love your wives, just as Christ also loved the church and gave Himself for her." (Ephesians 5:25)

The Greek word here for love is agapaō (ἀγαπάω), self-giving, sacrificial love. Paul defines this love not as affection but as death-to-self leadership.

He is restoring what Adam lost. Now we turn to the command given to the wife: "Wives, submit to your own husbands, as to the Lord" (Ephesians 5:22). Once again, the word is hypotassō, a willing alignment with divine order, not forced subordination.

Paul is restoring what Eve lost: trust-based partnership instead of control-based governance. The man is not commanded to dominate; he is commanded to die. The woman is not commanded to disappear; she is invited to realign in trust. This is not oppression. This is the redemption of order.

Paul then anchors marriage in the highest possible pattern, Christ and the Church. "For no one ever hated his own flesh, but nourishes and cherishes it, just as the Lord does the church" (Ephesians 5:29). Christ does not dominate the Church; He gives Himself for her. And the Church does not govern Christ; she aligns with Him. This is Eden restored without the serpent, authority without tyranny, partnership without rebellion, leadership without fear, and submission without loss of identity.

When Power Has No Target

One of the most painful realities in many marriages is when a woman carries enormous capacity, but no defined mission to support. Her strength has nowhere to pour. Her discernment has no structure. Her endurance is consumed by survival instead of construction.

This is where burnout grows.
This is where resentment forms.

This is where emotional distance begins.

But when her power becomes aligned with purpose, something holy ignites. She becomes a builder of destiny, not merely a manager of dysfunction.

Partnership Was Always God's Intention

From the beginning, marriage was never intended to be:
One leading and one following in fear.
One commanding and one complying in silence.

It was meant to be:
One assigned by God.
One empowered by God.
Two aligned in covenant.
Two building under heaven.

The man carries the mandate.
The woman carries the multiplier.
Together, they carry the future.

This is the power of ezer.

CHAPTER 4

SUBMISSION, SAFETY, AND ABUSE: RESTORING WHAT FEAR HAS DISTORTED

When Holy Language Is Used to Justify Harm

Few biblical words have been more abused than the word submission. What was designed by God to be a posture of strength has, in many settings, been twisted into a tool of fear. What was meant to represent order has been used to excuse terror. What was meant to bring protection has, in tragic cases, been used to justify control, domination, and violence.

This chapter exists because truth must do more than inspire, it must protect.

Many women have been told, "Stay and submit," when what they were enduring was not leadership, but abuse. Many men have hidden behind spiritual language to avoid confronting sin. And many marriages have been spiritually silenced under teachings that confused order with oppression.

Scripture never authorizes the violation of covenant through harm. God never sanctifies brutality. Christ never leads through terror.

Submission Was Never Meant to Cost You Your Safety

Biblical submission was never designed to strip a woman of her voice, her will, or her safety. The God who created order is the same God who created refuge. Throughout Scripture, God reveals

Himself as a protector of the vulnerable, a defender of the oppressed, and a judge against violence.

"The Lord is a refuge for the oppressed, a stronghold in times of trouble." (Psalm 9:9)

"Rescue the weak and the needy; deliver them from the hand of the wicked." (Psalm 82:4)

These are not poetic ideals. They are divine standards.

Submission never means:
- Enduring physical violence
- Absorbing emotional terror
- Remaining silent under domination
- Accepting spiritual manipulation
- Or being trapped in cycles of degradation

A woman is never called by God to support sin under the banner of order. Submission is not alignment with destruction; it is alignment with mission under Christ. Any teaching that demands a woman remain in harm, silence, or sin for the sake of "order" has already departed from the heart of God.

God never asks anyone to preserve what Christ came to redeem. True biblical submission only exists where Christ remains the center and where righteousness, safety, and truth are upheld. Order without Christ at the center is not order at all, it is simply organized dysfunction.

This is why the difference between authority and abuse must be clearly understood. Authority is always connected to accountability. Abuse is always connected to control without consequence. Christ never exercised authority to elevate Himself; He exercised authority to give Himself. "The Son of Man did not come to be served, but to serve, and to give His life as a ransom for many" (Matthew 20:28).

Any leadership that crushes rather than covers, that wounds rather than washes, that threatens rather than shepherds, has already departed from the nature of Christ. Where Christ rules, authority restores. Where abuse rules, fear replaces love and control replaces covenant.

Abuse is not:
- Harsh moments in conflict
- Raised voices in emotional exchanges
- Or seasons of dysfunction being confronted

Abuse is:
- The consistent misuse of power
- The systematic removal of safety
- The ongoing cultivation of fear
- The repeated violation of dignity

And none of this is ever sanctified by Scripture.

Why Fear Destroys the Architecture of Covenant

Covenant requires safety to breathe. Fear suffocates covenant at the foundation. No real submission can exist where terror rules. No real trust can grow where threat persists. No real partnership can form in an atmosphere of intimidation.

Perfect love does not coexist with fear; it expels it. Scripture says plainly, "There is no fear in love; but perfect love casts out fear" (1 John 4:18). This means fear is not a tool of God's government, it is a signal that God's order has been violated.

When fear dominates a home, covenant stops functioning and survival takes over. And survival is never the same thing as faith. Where fear rules, people shrink. Where love rules, people become. And no marriage can reflect the heart of Christ while being governed by fear.

When the Man Leaves His Place Under Christ

Biblical order only works when every layer is properly aligned.

Christ → Man → Woman

But when the man leaves his place under Christ, morally, spiritually, emotionally, or physically, he does not drag the woman out from under Christ with him.

A woman's ultimate allegiance is never to dysfunction; it is always to God. The moment a man abandons Christ's authority through violence, addiction, domination, sexual sin, rage, or spiritual abuse, he forfeits the spiritual right to demand alignment in those areas. God never requires a woman to follow a man into sin to be called submissive. Submission is never obedience to destruction; it is alignment to righteousness under Christ.

Wherever sin governs, Christ's authority has already been rejected. And where Christ's authority is rejected, blind allegiance is not submission, it is compromise. God's order never asks a woman to endanger her soul, her body, or her conscience in the name of covenant.

Why Silence Is Sometimes Not Submission, But Survival

Many women are quiet not because they are submitted, but because they are afraid. Silence can indeed be wisdom, but it can also be trauma. God never calls fear obedience. Fear-driven silence is not submission; it is evidence that danger has entered the environment. Submission only thrives in safety. It withers in threat.

This is why true healing must always address atmosphere before alignment can ever be restored. Where fear is removed, trust can grow. And where trust is restored, alignment can finally become real.

Healing Does Not Mean Pretending the Past Never Happened

Many couples attempt reconciliation by ignoring history. But you cannot heal what you refuse to name. True restoration requires:
- Confession without justification
- Accountability without defensiveness
- Boundaries without punishment
- And truth without retaliation

Abuse cannot be healed through forgetting. It is healed through truth, repentance, and transformation.

Forgiveness is powerful, but it is not a substitute for repentance. Reconciliation is sacred, but it is never forced. Restoration is holy, but it is never rushed.

God's Heart Has Always Been Protection First

The God of Scripture consistently reveals Himself as:
"The defender of the fatherless and the widow." (Psalm 68:5)

He positions Himself on the side of the vulnerable. This is not secondary to His nature, it is His nature. Any teaching on marriage, submission, or order that contradicts this revelation is already distorted.

God's order never crushes.
God's order always covers.

Where Restoration Truly Begins

When abuse has existed, restoration does not begin with submission, it begins with safety. It may require separation for a season, if necessary, the establishment of real accountability, counsel that confronts both trauma and sin, deliverance where bondage remains, and, above all, the visible fruit of genuine repentance. Only after trust has been patiently and consistently rebuilt can alignment even be discussed again. Order cannot be restored where terror still reigns. Fear and faith do not grow in the same soil, and no covenant can function rightly where safety has not first been reestablished.

The Goal Is Not Power, It Is Protection

Marriage was never designed to be a contest of dominance; it was designed to be a sanctuary of partnership. The headship of a man was never meant to function as a throne, it was meant to serve as a covering.

And the alignment of a wife was never meant to be a burden, it was meant to be safety expressed through strength. Anything else may wear the language of religion, but it is not biblical marriage. It is spiritual distortion.

Fear entered the marriage relationship through sin, but redemption restores safety through Christ. Abuse distorts identity, but redemption restores dignity. Domination fractures trust, but redemption rebuilds covenant. This is the work Christ came to accomplish, not only to secure heaven after death, but to heal the home in the present.

The gospel was never meant to stop at forgiveness alone; it was always meant to reach into relationships, to restore what fear corrupted and to rebuild what sin fractured, beginning at the altar of the home.

CHAPTER 5

WHEN TWO PURPOSEFUL PEOPLE NEVER DEFINE ONE SHARED MISSION

The Quiet Fracture That Looks Like Success

One of the most subtle fractures in marriage is not caused by sin, betrayal, or abuse. It is caused by something far quieter and far more deceptive: two purposeful people who never define one shared mission.

From the outside, these marriages often look successful. Both husband and wife are driven. Both are productive. Both are gifted. Both are busy. Schedules are full. Calendars are packed. Responsibilities multiply. But beneath all the motion, something essential is missing direction as one.

They are moving.
They are just not moving together.

This is how many marriages become exhausted without becoming united.

Individual Calling Cannot Replace Corporate Assignment

A man may be called to ministry, business, leadership, education, or innovation. A woman may be called to intercession, creativity, influence, teaching, counseling, leadership, or entrepreneurship. Both may be genuinely anointed. Both may be sincerely obedient to God. Yet still, the marriage can feel strained, hollow, and disconnected.

Why?

Because individual calling was never meant to replace shared assignment.

Calling answers the question, "Why do I exist?"
Marriage answers the question, "Why do we exist together?"

When these two questions remain disconnected, tension is inevitable. The couple becomes a house with two altars instead of one. Decisions become negotiations instead of agreements. Schedules become competitive instead of cooperative. Energy becomes divided instead of multiplied.

They love each other.
But they are not building together.

When Purpose Is Not Unified, Life Becomes Transactional

In the absence of a shared mission, marriage slowly shifts from covenant to transaction. Instead of asking, "What are we building together?" couples begin asking, "What am I getting from this?" Service becomes conditional. Sacrifice becomes negotiated. Effort becomes measured. Commitment becomes performance-based.

Without shared mission, every sacrifice feels like loss, every delay feels like unfairness, every compromise feels one-sided, and every hardship feels meaningless. But when mission is shared, sacrifice becomes investment, delay becomes preparation, hardship becomes training, and pressure becomes forging. Purpose gives suffering meaning. Without it, endurance feels pointless.

Many couples today are not disconnected because they lack activity; they are disconnected because they lack alignment. They move from task to task, obligation to obligation, responsibility to responsibility, but they no longer move with each other at the center. This is why some homes are full of motion but empty of intimacy. They are efficient. They are productive. They are responsible. But they are not connected at the level of assignment. And movement without agreement will always lead to exhaustion long before it ever leads to fulfillment.

When the Woman Is Powerful but Underutilized

In many marriages, the woman carries tremendous strength, intelligence, insight, and discernment, but she has never been clearly invited into a shared mission. Her capacity remains vast, but undefined. She supports effort instead of assignment. She manages survival instead of building legacy.

And when power is present without purpose, frustration grows.

This is where many women become weary, disappointed, and internally disconnected, not because they lack devotion, but because they were never given a target worthy of their strength.

A woman was designed to multiply purpose.
But she cannot multiply what was never defined.

When the Woman Withdraws from Partnership

There is another side to the conversation that must be spoken with equal clarity and equal honor. Just as a woman can be underutilized by a man who refuses to see her, she can also withdraw herself from partnership because of insecurity, fear, disappointment, or wounded trust. And when this happens, the marriage does not lose conflict, it loses momentum.

If God brought a woman into covenant with a man, He did not bring an under-equipped partner. He brought a fully endowed ezer. The Hebrew word ezer does not describe an assistant lacking strength. It is the same word used in Scripture to describe God as Israel's helper. It speaks of one who comes alongside with power, with reinforcement, with supply, and with strategic support. God never assigns inadequacy to covenant. He only assigns purpose.

This means a woman was never designed to merely observe her husband's mission from a distance. She was designed to undergird it, to strengthen it, to carry it with him, and to help it move from vision to reality. And because this empowerment is God-given, it is not dependent on emotion. It is not revoked by disappointment. It is not canceled by seasons of fear. What God placed within her remains, even when she feels unsure of herself.

Yet insecurity can quietly convince a woman that she has nothing to offer. Past wounds can whisper that her voice does not matter. Disappointment can persuade her that engaging again is too risky. And slowly, she may begin to refuse partnership, not through rebellion, but through retreat. She becomes present physically while remaining absent purposefully. She supports logistically but withholds spiritually. She participates in survival but avoids vision.

This is not humility. It is fear wearing the language of caution.

A woman is not asked to partner because she feels confident. She is asked to partner because God made her capable. Her strength does not originate in her emotional certainty. It originates in her divine design. And no season of insecurity negates God's original intention when He said, "It is not good that the man should be alone."

Partnership is not optional in covenant. It is essential. And when a woman refuses to engage because she feels inadequate, she unknowingly contradicts what God declared true when He formed her to be ezer. Feelings may fluctuate, but design does not.

This does not mean she ignores wisdom. It does not mean she suppresses discernment. It does not mean she partners with destruction. But it does mean that when God has joined her to a man under His authority, she carries a real responsibility to show up fully, not just survive quietly. To contribute, not just coexist. To reinforce, not just endure.

Do Not Control What You Were Called to Fortify

A woman does not become powerful by taking over a man's mission. She becomes powerful by fortifying it. And she does not lose herself in that process, she finds herself aligned with why she was created. God never misassigns help. If He joined you to a man, He fully equipped you to stand with him.

Yet one of the most subtle dangers in marriage is when empowerment quietly mutates into control. This often happens not because a woman is malicious, but because she becomes convinced, through fear, disappointment, or distrust, that her husband is incapable of carrying his own mandate. When that belief takes root, she may begin to "help" by teaching, directing, correcting, enforcing, or overriding. What began as support slowly becomes supervision. What once was partnership becomes governance.

This is where distortion enters.

When a woman views her husband as incapable of his own God-given assignment, she may feel justified in steering his life with pressure instead of prayer, manipulation instead of trust, control instead of covering. She may believe that because she can see more clearly, move more efficiently, or act more decisively, she must therefore take over. But in doing so, she does not merely reshape a household, she begins to misrepresent the marriage, misrepresent Christ, misrepresent the Kingdom, and misrepresent herself.

Control is never a fruit of faith. It is always a symptom of fear.

Instead of undergirding, she enforces.
Instead of reinforcing, she redirects.
Instead of trusting God's work in her husband, she substitutes herself for it.

And slowly, the man is no longer being strengthened, he is being managed. He is no longer growing through responsibility, he is shrinking under supervision. What was meant to be a mission carried together becomes a path dictated by one.

This is particularly dangerous when the calling requires faith.

I have personally known women who have forbidden their husbands to enter into God-given callings because those callings required risk, sacrifice, and total dependency on God for provision. Some men were prevented from starting businesses because the unknown felt too threatening. Others were blocked from entering ministerial callings because the lifestyle of faith felt too unstable. In these moments, fear dressed itself as wisdom. Caution dressed itself as prudence. Control dressed itself as protection.

But protection that cancels obedience is no longer protection, it is obstruction.

A woman never dishonors herself by trusting God with her husband's calling. But she does dishonor the design of covenant when she replaces trust with control. She was not created to govern the man's assignment. She was created to fortify it. She does not give direction to his obedience, she gives strength to his obedience.

They Shall Be One

This does not mean she has no voice. It does not mean she lacks discernment. It does not mean she ignores red flags or partners with destruction. But it does mean that when God assigns a man a mission, a woman must be careful not to assign herself as the Holy Spirit over it.

Control does not accelerate God's will, it restricts it.

And here is the deeper truth that must be faced with humility: when a woman feels the need to control a man's obedience to God, it often reveals that she is afraid of the cost of his obedience. Faith will always threaten control because faith removes outcomes from human hands and places them in God's.

Partnership trusts God.
Control replaces Him.

True ezer does not dominate. It fortifies.
True partnership does not override. It reinforces.
True covenant does not steer by fear. It stands by faith.

A woman is never more powerful than when she strengthens what God is building in her husband instead of reshaping it according to her anxieties. And a man is never more empowered than when he knows his wife is standing behind him in faith rather than standing over him in fear.

God never misassigns help.

If He joined you to a man, He fully equipped you, not to control what He called him to carry, but to strengthen him as he carries it.

When the Man Labors Without Being Reinforced

Likewise, many men work relentlessly, pursue responsibility, and carry obligation, but without the strength of a fully aligned partner reinforcing the direction. They hold pressure internally. They absorb weight silently. They endure stress alone.

Many couples are leading, but they are not being multiplied. They are expending effort, carrying responsibility, and shouldering pressure, yet what they produce feels limited to maintenance rather than multiplication. This creates fatigue without fulfillment, labor without legacy.

Leadership was never meant to be carried alone, and marriage was never designed to function as a solo assignment shared by two tired people. It was meant to be a multiplying force.

A marriage can survive without a shared mission, but it can never fully build without one. Survival asks only, "How do we get through this?" but mission asks a far greater question: "What are we becoming through this?" Survival maintains what already exists. Mission multiplies what has been planted. Survival preserves. Mission advances. Survival focuses on stability, but mission gives birth to legacy. One keeps the structure standing; the other gives the structure meaning.

Everything begins to change the moment a couple finally defines why they are together, what they are building, who they are called to serve, what problem in the earth they were designed to solve, and what legacy they intend to leave behind.

When those questions are answered with clarity and unity, something supernatural begins to occur. Arguments decrease because direction increases. Confusion fades because purpose sharpens. Energy multiplies because effort is unified. Sacrifice becomes joyful because it is no longer wasted. The questions shift from, "What do I need from you?" to, "What are we building together?" And that is the moment marriage shifts from maintenance to movement.

Shared mission is the bridge between love and legacy. Love sustains a home, but mission gives that home a future. Without mission, children drift, vision fragments, momentum slows, and joy diminishes. But with mission, children inherit purpose, sacrifice gains meaning, identity becomes structured, and direction becomes generational. Shared mission is what turns romance into responsibility, affection into assignment, and union into legacy.

Why Many Marriages Fight Over Small Things

Many of the conflicts that tear at daily life, money, time, in-laws, schedules, priorities, and fatigue, are rarely the true problem. They are symptoms of something deeper: the absence of a clearly defined and mutually agreed-upon "why." When purpose is unclear, everything begins to feel personal. Every disagreement feels threatening. Every compromise feels costly, because there is no larger story those sacrifices belong to. Without shared purpose, even small tensions feel heavy and unresolved.

But when purpose becomes settled, everything begins to shift. Decisions become directional instead of defensive. Disagreements become manageable instead of overwhelming. Differences become contributions instead of threats. Clarity of purpose does not eliminate conflict, but it transforms the way conflict is interpreted. Differences stop being signs of division and begin to function as complementary strengths.

This reveals the hidden question every marriage must eventually answer. It is not simply, "Are we in love?" It is, "Do we know why we are together?" It is not merely, "Are we compatible?" but, "Are we aligned?" And it is not, "Are we busy?" but, "Are we building?" Because busyness can distract a marriage for years, but only purpose can sustain it for a lifetime.

The Invitation of This Chapter

This chapter is not calling couples to abandon individual calling. It is calling them to merge it into shared assignment. It is inviting husbands and wives to sit together, not just in affection, but in direction. To move beyond survival into construction. To stop merely living and start building something that will outlive them.

Because the goal of marriage is not just companionship.

It is legacy under God.

CHAPTER 6
CALLING WITHOUT CONFUSION: HER MISSION & HIS HEADSHIP IN GOD'S DESIGN

We live in a cultural moment that frequently asks a different question than Scripture asks. Instead of beginning with "What is God's order?", modern ideology often begins with Who is more gifted? Who is more visible? Who earns more? Who has the greater platform? And from that framework, many conclude that whichever spouse appears more influential must therefore hold the governing mandate within the marriage.

This is where profound confusion enters covenant.

There are women with extraordinary callings. Women who preach to nations. Women who build global businesses. Women who carry apostolic, prophetic, educational, medical, legal, and entrepreneurial authority. Scripture has never been threatened by strong women. Deborah, Huldah, Esther, Priscilla, Phoebe, Mary Magdalene, Lydia, God has always entrusted immense weight to women. The question is not whether a woman can carry calling. The question is whether calling ever reorders covenant headship.

And biblically, it does not.

Calling determines assignment.
Covenant determines order.

A woman's public influence does not negate God's private design. A woman may lead thousands and still be ordered within one. She may speak into nations and still choose alignment in her home.

Visibility is not headship. Giftedness is not governmental order. Impact does not cancel design.

Genesis never presents two parallel heads competing for authority. It presents one man formed first, and then a woman formed from him, not beneath him in worth, but ordered with him in function. The woman is called ezer, not the mission originator within covenant, but the mission fortifier. She is not lesser. She is not passive. But she is positioned in support of the man's assignment within covenant structure.

This is where modern ideology collides with divine pattern.

Contemporary culture teaches that whoever is most capable should lead. Scripture teaches that whoever is positioned by God carries order. Culture teaches that strength defines headship. Scripture teaches that responsibility before God defines headship. Culture teaches that power determines authority. Scripture teaches that sacrifice reveals authority.

A woman does not lose power because she aligns. She focuses power.

Even in rare public exceptions, such as Deborah, the order of male headship in Israel was never canceled; it was exposed as temporarily abdicated. God did not change the design. He confronted the absence of ordered leadership. Deborah herself affirmed that Barak was the military head. She did not seize the pattern, she summoned it back into place.

Here is the truth that must be spoken plainly and without apology:

A woman having a powerful calling does not mean she carries covenant headship.

Headship is not about gifting.
It is not about income.
It is not about charisma.
It is not about success.

It is about spiritual accountability before God for the covering of the marriage.

At the same time, Scripture never asks a woman to shrink her calling to protect a man's insecurity. A healthy marriage never requires a woman to abandon what God entrusted to her. But it does require that her power operate inside covenant order, not above it.

A woman is never called to dominate a man because she is gifted.
A man is never called to suppress a woman because he is threatened.

When a woman's calling outpaces a man's maturity, the answer is not control, it is intercession.

When a man's insecurity rises in the face of a woman's strength, the answer is not suppression, it is growth.

The goal is not competition.
The goal is completion.

The Kingdom question is not, Who is stronger?
It is always, Who is ordered?

A woman can thunder in the pulpit and still rest in covenant alignment at home.

A man can quietly serve and still carry the weight of headship before God.

The question is never who is more gifted.

The question is always: Who is answering for this union before the Lord?

A Woman's Responsibility: The Power of Alignment

Biblical submission is not weakness, it is power rightly positioned. It is not silence, it is strength disciplined toward purpose. A woman is not called to disappear in covenant. She is called to deploy her full measure of grace, discernment, wisdom, creativity, and spiritual authority in a way that fortifies the mission God has entrusted to the man she is joined to.

The woman is not placed in the marriage to diminish herself. She is placed there as ezer, a divine helper, a strength that comes alongside, a force that upholds what would otherwise collapse under weight. Scripture uses this same word to describe God Himself as Israel's helper. This means the woman was never meant to be ornamental. She was meant to be formidable in support.

But with that power comes responsibility.

A woman's influence in marriage is immense. She sets emotional climate. She shapes internal tone. She either magnifies faith or multiplies fear. She either steadies vision or unsettles it. Her words do not merely communicate, they prophesy atmosphere.

This is why Scripture calls a wife to align, not because she lacks discernment, but because unchecked discernment easily becomes governance. When a woman shifts from strengthening to steering, from advising to overriding, from undergirding to over-managing, the order Christ established in the home begins to fracture, not because she is evil, but because her power has lost alignment.

A woman's responsibility is not to take the man's mission and reshape it into her own version of safety. It is to stand with him while

God shapes him into the man capable of carrying the mission. This requires faith. This requires restraint. This requires trust.

Control often wears the mask of wisdom. But wisdom comes from peace, not fear. When fear governs a woman's counsel, fear of lack, fear of instability, fear of loss, fear of failure, her words may sound practical but they are no longer prophetic. They may sound cautious but they are no longer courageous. And slowly, partnership turns into regulation.

A woman is never called by God to control what she is called to cover.

Remember, if a woman views her husband as incapable of his own mandate, she will feel driven to "teach him," manage him, redirect him, or restrain him. And without realizing it, she may become the dominant force in the home, not as a partner, but as a substitute head. This distorts covenant, misrepresents Christ and the Church, and fractures the spiritual architecture of marriage.

Again, some women, even with sincere hearts, have forbidden their husbands from entering God-given callings because the calling threatened comfort, security, or financial predictability. Businesses were delayed. Ministries were aborted. Faith assignments were restrained. Not because the husband was wrong, but because fear was governing the partnership.

This is not undergirding.
This is obstruction disguised as protection.

A woman's responsibility is not to enforce her will on God's will for her husband. It is to stand in faith while God transforms him into the man required for the assignment. She does not lead him by pressure. She leads him by presence. She does not move him by fear. She reinforces him by faith.

When a woman aligns rightly, she becomes terrifying to darkness, because she now operates without competition, without insecurity, without control. Her strength becomes pure. Her counsel becomes clear. Her support becomes supernatural.

And alignment does not require silence. A godly wife speaks. She discerns. She warns. She advises. She intercedes. But she does so without usurping. She does so without overriding. She does so without dismantling the order that gives her influence its greatest power.

True submission does not erase a woman's identity.
It deploys it accurately.

She does not become less.
She becomes joined.

And when she chooses faith over fear, partnership over control, and trust over management, her presence no longer competes with headship, it completes it.

Is the Man Truly the Head of the Wife?

Few biblical teachings have been more disputed, reinterpreted, or emotionally charged in modern times than the claim that the man is the head of the wife. Some reject it as cultural. Others as oppressive. Others as outdated. Many attempt to neutralize it by redefining it beyond recognition. The controversy is not merely theological, it is cultural, emotional, and personal.

So the question must be asked plainly and answered honestly:

"Does Scripture actually teach that the man is the head of the wife?"

The answer, when approached without fear, tradition, or ideology, is yes. But what Scripture means by head is radically different from what culture assumes.

"For the husband is head of the wife, as also Christ is head of the church." (Ephesians 5:23)

The word "head" here is the Greek kephalē, meaning the governing point, the one who bears responsibility, the source under God for covering. It does not mean tyrant. It does not mean dictator. It does not mean superior being. It means **the one who answers to God for what flows beneath him.**

Headship in Scripture is always about accountability before God, not dominance over people.

Paul reinforces this again:

"But I want you to know that the head of every man is Christ, the head of woman is man, and the head of Christ is God."
(1 Corinthians 11:3)

This establishes a four-layered order:
God → Christ → Man → Woman

And even Christ Himself is under the Father in functional order, without any loss of equality. The Son is not less than the Father in worth, power, or deity, yet He submits in role. This single truth dismantles the modern lie that submission equals inferiority.

Order in Scripture is about function, not value.

Genesis supports this order long before the Fall:
"For Adam was formed first, then Eve." (1 Timothy 2:13)

This means headship did not originate in sin. It existed before sin. The Fall distorted it, but did not create it. So why the resistance?

Because modern thinking confuses:
- Headship with dominance
- Authority with control
- Leadership with superiority
- Order with oppression

But Christ redefines every one of these. Jesus, the ultimate Head, said:
"The Son of Man did not come to be served, but to serve, and to give His life as a ransom for many." (Matthew 20:28)

So if Christ defines headship by self-giving, then any man who uses headship to control, silence, intimidate, manipulate, or dominate is already violating the Head he claims to represent.

Biblical headship means:
- Sacrifice, not entitlement
- Responsibility, not dominance
- Covering, not coercion
- Accountability, not autonomy

A man is not head because he is better.
He is head because he is held responsible by God.

This is why the command to men is far heavier than the command to women:

"Husbands, love your wives, just as Christ also loved the church and gave Himself for her." (Ephesians 5:25)

Women are called to align.
Men are called to fully give of themselves.

Not Merely Genesis, A Pauline Revelation in Christ

What Paul reveals here is not merely a Genesis structure being carried forward. This is not just creation order being restated. This is New Covenant revelation through Christ and the Church.

"This is a great mystery, but I speak concerning Christ and the church." (Ephesians 5:32)

Genesis reveals pattern.
Paul reveals purpose.

Adam and Eve were not merely the first couple, they were the first prophetic shadow of Christ and His Bride. Paul is not arguing from biology, he is unveiling Christological order.

So this is not **Old Covenant structure**.
This is **New Covenant revelation** unveiled backward into creation.

This Is Not an Old Covenant Argument

Some will try to dismiss this by saying, "That's just Old Covenant thinking." But Paul is not writing Torah, he is writing to Spirit-filled believers under grace.

Ephesians is not Moses.
Corinthians is not Sinai.

Paul does not root marriage order in law, he roots it in Christ and the Church. And if Christ is still the Head and the Church is still the Bride, the revelation cannot be outdated.

Christ did not erase order.
He redeemed it.

Why This Matters for Real Marriages

This chapter is not about gender rivalry.
It is not about platform wars.
It is not about suppressing women or inflating men.

It is about restoring:
- Order without oppression
- Strength without domination
- Calling without confusion

When a woman understands her power without trying to replace divine order, she becomes terrifying to darkness.

When a man embraces headship without abandoning tenderness, he becomes a covering instead of a threat.

This is not hierarchy of worth.
This is harmony of function.

This is how Christ and the Church are revealed, not through domination, but through ordered love.

A Man's Responsibility: The Weight of Headship

Biblical headship is not privilege, it is burden. It is not authority for comfort, it is authority for covering. The man does not stand as head because he is superior. He stands as head because he is assigned first to answer to God for what happens beneath him. Headship is not about having the final word, it is about bearing the final accountability.

A man is not called to be the loudest voice in the home. He is called to be the first to repent, the first to forgive, the first to sacrifice, and the first to stand between danger and the people God entrusted to him. His authority is never measured by how much control he exercises, but by how much responsibility he absorbs.

The New Testament does not tell men to rule their homes. It tells them to give themselves for them.

"Husbands, love your wives, just as Christ also loved the church and gave Himself for her." (Ephesians 5:25)

This single sentence defines everything headship is. Christ did not establish His authority by demanding submission. He established it by giving Himself completely. And no man can **claim Christlike headship** while **avoiding Christlike sacrifice**.

A man's responsibility is first spiritual before it is ever practical. He is called to be under authority before he ever functions in authority. If he is not submitted to Christ in character, he cannot rightly represent Christ in covenant. A man who refuses correction, rejects accountability, or avoids repentance is not exercising headship, he is abandoning it.

Remember the order: God → Christ → Man → Woman

Therefore:
"When the man's head is at the feet of Jesus, then he can properly function as the head of his wife"

Headship means a man takes responsibility even when the failure was mutual. It means he does not hide in passivity when conflict rises. It means he does not weaponize silence, distance, or intimidation when he feels unsure. It means he does not hand leadership to his wife because he is afraid to grow.

A man's presence in a marriage is meant to feel like protection, not pressure. His leadership should feel like safety, not threat. His direction should feel like clarity, not confusion. His love should feel like covering, not control.

If a wife cannot rest under her husband's leadership, the man must ask hard questions, not of her resistance, but of his own representation. Am I walking with God privately? Am I honest when no one is watching? Am I consistent in character? Am I growing in humility? Am I carrying responsibility emotionally as well as financially? Am I listening without defensiveness? Am I building safety, or merely expecting alignment?

Men are **never called to demand submission**. They are called to **create an environment where submission feels safe** because love is consistent.

This is why Scripture never commands women to submit to weak character. It commands women to submit to Christ-expressing leadership. And no man should ever weaponize verses to extract alignment while refusing the weight of obedience himself.

A man's responsibility is to:
- Lead without performing
- Provide without pride
- Protect without intimidation
- Decide without domination
- Stand without disappearing
- Serve without resentment
- Sacrifice without keeping score

This is not masculine ego.
This is mature sonship.

And when a man embraces this responsibility, not perfectly, but sincerely, something shifts in the home. Alignment becomes possible because trust has been cultivated. Partnership becomes joyful because leadership is no longer threatening. The home becomes a place of rest instead of negotiation.

When a man takes his place under Christ, the entire house finds its place under God.

Joint Responsibility: What They Carry Together

While headship and alignment establish order, joint responsibility establishes movement. Order gives a marriage structure, but shared responsibility gives it momentum. This is where the covenant stops being theoretical and becomes functional. The man carries headship before God. The woman carries strength alongside him. But both carry the weight of the house together.

Marriage was never designed to function as a hierarchy of effort. It was designed to operate as a union of stewardship. The man is not responsible for vision alone. The woman is not responsible for atmosphere alone. Both are responsible for:
- The health of the home
- The protection of the covenant
- The culture of the marriage
- The direction of the family
- The spiritual climate of the household
- And the legacy they are building

No spouse gets to outsource responsibility to the other and still call it partnership.

Joint responsibility means that neither spouse hides behind role language to avoid growth. A man cannot excuse emotional absence by saying, "I provide." A woman cannot excuse control by saying, "I care." Provision without presence fractures intimacy. Care without trust fractures order.

Both are called to grow.
Both are called to heal.
Both are called to repent.
Both are called to mature.

A marriage becomes powerful when neither spouse is the perpetual victim and neither is the perpetual villain. They stop asking, "Who is wrong?" and begin asking, "What is ours to own?"

Joint responsibility means they guard each other's dignity in public and confront each other's issues in private. It means they do not weaponize trauma. They do not rehearse failures in moments of anger. They do not expose weakness to win arguments. They become keepers of each other's humanity, not prosecutors of each other's mistakes.

It also means that spiritual life is not delegated. The man cannot carry prayer alone. The woman cannot carry discernment alone. One cannot become the "spiritual one" while the other becomes the bystander. They intercede together. They seek God together. They repent together. They align together.

This is where marriage becomes truly apostolic instead of merely romantic.

Joint responsibility also governs how conflict is handled. They stop fighting for supremacy and start fighting for the marriage itself. They no longer make each other the enemy. They identify the problem as the enemy. They stop keeping score and start keeping covenant.

This is the sacred shift from:
"Me versus you"
to
"Us versus what threatens what God joined."

When one spouse weakens, the other does not exploit it, they **cover it**.
When one falls, the other does not weaponize it, they **restore it**.
When one doubts, the other does not mock it, they **carry faith for both** until belief returns.

This is the law of covenant: what touches one touches both.

Joint responsibility means neither spouse lives as a guest in the marriage. Both live as builders. Both invest. Both protect. Both initiate. Both take risks. Both bear consequence. Both share reward.

This is how two truly become one, not by erasing difference, but by sharing destiny.

CHAPTER 7

THE CLASHING OF NORMALS: WHEN TWO HISTORIES COLLIDE IN COVENANT

You Didn't Just Marry a Person, You Married a Formation

Every couple enters marriage believing they are choosing a person. What very few realize is that they are also choosing a formation. Long before two people ever meet, they have already been shaped by a home, a culture, a language of love, and a model of conflict. By the time they fall in love, much of who they are has already been quietly formed in the background of their upbringing.

This is why marriage is not the merging of two blank slates. It is the collision of two worlds.

You may not have married their family, but you certainly married what their family shaped them to be. Their reflexes, their emotional responses, their tone in conflict, their expectations around affection, money, discipline, communication, rest, anger, silence, celebration, and disappointment were all learned somewhere. Most of it was never consciously chosen. It was absorbed.

This is what creates what many couples experience as the great surprise of marriage. They say, "You've changed," when in reality, they are simply encountering the version of their spouse that pressure reveals.

Marriage Does Not Create the Fracture, It Reveals It

Many people enter marriage believing love will erase difference. They assume affection will override history and feelings will neutralize formation. But marriage does not erase culture. It exposes it. It does not eliminate patterns. It magnifies them. It does not dissolve reflexes. It activates them under pressure.

This is why the early years of marriage often feel disorienting. The very things that once felt charming now feel confusing. The differences that once seemed small now feel immense. The habits that once felt harmless now feel personal. What changed was not the person. What changed was the level of proximity and pressure.

Pressure does not create who we are. It reveals who we already became.

Why "Irreconcilable Differences" Is Usually a Misdiagnosis

Many marriages eventually reach a place where the phrase "irreconcilable differences" is spoken. It sounds dignified. It sounds reasonable. It sounds final. But in reality, most differences were never reconciled in the first place because they were never understood.

The differences did not suddenly appear. They were always there, when you met, when you dated, when you got engaged, and when you spoke your vows. What changed was not the difference. What changed was the grace for the difference.

In the early days, love covers much. In the early days, patience flows freely. In the early days, curiosity exceeds judgment. But as disappointment accumulates, fatigue sets in, expectations go unmet, and wounds go unhealed, the very same differences that once felt manageable begin to feel unbearable.

Differences only become "irreconcilable" when honor quietly erodes.

How Family Culture Becomes the Hidden Third Voice in Marriage

Every home has a language. Some homes speak through affection. Others speak through silence. Some homes resolve conflict through conversation. Others bury it through avoidance. Some homes express anger loudly. Others express it indirectly. Some homes celebrate openly. Others restrain joy.

When two people marry, these invisible languages come with them. Long after the wedding day, these voices continue to speak in moments of stress, fear, disappointment, and tension. This is why many couples find themselves reacting in ways they do not fully understand.

They say things they do not mean.
They withdraw when they want to pursue.
They pursue when they should pause.
They explode when they should speak.
They shut down when they should stay present.

And often they are shocked by their own behavior.

What they do not realize is that their nervous system is speaking the language it learned long before their marriage began.

The Danger of Unspoken Expectations

One of the most destructive dynamics in marriage is not disagreement, it is assumption. We assume our spouse knows what we mean. We assume they should value what we value. We assume they should react how we would react. We assume the way we were raised is the way we think things should be done.

But what we call "common sense" is often just familiar sense.

When expectations remain unspoken, disappointment becomes unavoidable. When disappointment is repeated, resentment grows quietly. And when resentment goes unaddressed, love becomes guarded instead of generous.

Many couples are **not fighting over what happened**. They are **fighting over what they assumed should have happened**.

Covenant Does Not Trap You in Your Past, It Authorizes You to Rewrite It

Here is where hope enters.

Marriage does not exist to imprison you in your upbringing. It exists to give you the authority to build a new culture together. You are not destined to repeat what shaped you; you are invited to redeem it. You are allowed to question what you inherited, to challenge what you observed, to outgrow what once defined you, and to heal what once wounded you. Marriage does not say, "You must remain who you were." It says, "You are free to become who you choose to build as one." This is not a betrayal of your parents, it is the stewardship of your future.

Every healthy marriage must eventually do the quiet, unseen work of renegotiating what feels normal. This work is not glamorous. It is not dramatic. It is rarely public. But it is absolutely essential. This is the work of learning how your spouse was formed long before you met them. It is the work of translating their reactions instead of judging them, of redefining habits together instead of defending them, and of deciding, intentionally and prayerfully, what kind of home you will build going forward.

Renegotiation happens through honest, vulnerable language. It sounds like saying, "This is how I learned to handle conflict," or, "This is why silence feels threatening to me." It sounds like, "This is why raised voices shut me down," and, "This is why money triggers fear for me," and, "This is why affection matters so deeply to me," and even, "This is why I retreat when I feel pressured." These conversations are not about blame; they are about understanding. And where understanding grows, compassion follows. This is how two histories stop competing and begin cooperating to form a new legacy.

When this kind of honesty becomes possible, hostility begins to dissolve. Compassion replaces confusion. Understanding displaces assumption. Grace begins to grow where judgment once lived.

Why Some People Fight and Others Freeze

Some people were raised in homes where anger was loud, expressive, and immediate. Others were raised in homes where anger was buried, avoided, and never named. When these two worlds collide in marriage, one spouse fights while the other freezes. One pursues while the other withdraws. One needs immediate resolution to feel safe, while the other needs space simply to survive the emotional intensity of the moment. Neither response is evil. Both are formed. The marriage does not become a battlefield because one person is wrong and the other is right, but because neither yet knows how to translate the other's emotional language.

This is why healing does not truly begin with demands for change. Real healing begins with curiosity. Not when a couple says, "What's wrong with you?" but when they learn to ask, "What happened to you?" Not when they accuse, "Why are you so difficult?" but when they begin to wonder, "What did you have to survive that trained you to react this way?" Curiosity opens doors that criticism never can. Understanding softens hearts where blame only hardens them. And when hearts are softened, transformation becomes possible without warfare.

From Collision to Construction

When the clashing of normals remains unaddressed, marriage becomes a cycle of misunderstanding. But when it is faced with humility, something powerful begins to happen. Differences stop being threats and begin to become tools. Diversity becomes strength. Contrast becomes balance.

What once collided can eventually complete.

But only when both husband and wife are willing to stop demanding that the other become familiar, and start committing to build something new together.

CHAPTER 8

WHEN YOUR SPOUSE STOPS BEING A SAFE PLACE

The Day Safety Quietly Leaves the Marriage

Most marriages do not lose safety in a single explosive moment. Safety usually leaves quietly. It slips out through repeated misunderstandings, unhealed disappointments, unmet expectations, and unresolved conflicts. Over time, what once felt welcoming begins to feel risky. What once felt safe begins to feel unpredictable. What once felt tender begins to feel tenderized.

At some point, one or both spouses realize they are editing their words. They are withholding thoughts. They are protecting themselves emotionally. They are choosing silence not because there is nothing to say, but because saying it no longer feels safe.

And that is the moment a marriage begins to suffer internally, even if everything still looks fine externally.

Why Honesty Is the First Casualty

Safety and truth live together. Where safety is present, truth flows freely. Where safety is threatened, truth becomes guarded.

Many husbands stop being honest not because they are deceptive by nature, but because they have learned through experience that honesty leads to explosion, humiliation, or prolonged conflict. Many wives stop being vulnerable not because they are manipulative, but because they have learned that honesty leads to dismissal, defensiveness, or emotional withdrawal.

So both learn a new skill: self-protection through silence.

This is how marriages drift into emotional distance while still sharing the same bed, the same roof, and the same responsibilities.

When Reactions Become More Dangerous Than the Truth

In many marriages, the danger is no longer the issue, it is the reaction to the issue.

A husband may be struggling internally and feel unable to speak because past honesty was met with rage, accusation, or emotional punishment. A wife may be struggling internally and remain silent because previous vulnerability was met with minimization, logic, or emotional detachment. Over time, both learn the same devastating lesson: the truth costs too much here. And so the truth becomes buried. But buried truth never heals, it only decomposes. What is hidden does not disappear; it decays beneath the surface, releasing toxins into the atmosphere of the relationship until distance feels safer than honesty and silence feels safer than connection.

The Difference Between Conflict and Unsafety

Conflict in marriage is not the problem, unsafety is. Healthy marriages argue. Healthy marriages disagree. Healthy marriages confront issues openly and directly. But unhealthy marriages make disagreement dangerous. When every conflict becomes a threat to stability, affection, or trust, the nervous system begins to associate honesty with danger. And when the body perceives danger, it instinctively defaults to survival behaviors: fight, flight, freeze, or fawn. At that point, conversations are no longer about resolution; they are about self-protection.

Marriage was never designed to be a survival environment. It was meant to be a sanctuary for the soul, a place where truth can be spoken without terror, where conflict can exist without catastrophe, and where disagreement does not threaten belonging. When safety is restored, conflict no longer destroys connection; it becomes the very tool through which intimacy, understanding, and trust are deepened.

Why Men Often Retreat and Women Often Explode

Many men were trained, explicitly or implicitly, to believe their worth is tied to performance, strength, and stability. When conflict surfaces, they often feel they are failing. Rather than engage emotionally, they retreat inward to preserve dignity and composure. Silence becomes their refuge.

Many women were trained, explicitly or implicitly, to value connection, emotional expression, and relational clarity. When conflict surfaces, they often feel abandonment, fear, or invisibility. Rather than retreat, they pursue through intensified emotion and urgency. Expression becomes their weapon and their cry.

So one retreats to survive.
The other pursues to survive.

Neither is evil.
Both are afraid.

And fear always warps communication.

When Truth Becomes a Weapon Instead of a Bridge

In some marriages, safety does not disappear through silence, it disappears through repeated emotional injury. Truth is spoken, but it is spoken with sharpness. Vulnerability is offered, but it is later weaponized. Weakness is revealed, but it reappears as ammunition in the next argument.

This is one of the deepest betrayals of safety.

When what was shared in trust becomes used in conflict, the heart learns a brutal lesson:

"Never be naked here again."

And once vulnerability dies, intimacy soon follows.

The Silent Agreement That Destroys Intimacy

Many couples unknowingly enter into a silent agreement:
"You don't press into my pain, and I won't press into yours."

On the surface, this feels peaceful.
In reality, it is emotional exile.

They coexist without collision.
They cooperate without communion.
They function without intimacy.

And they convince themselves this is maturity.

But what they have really built is a truce, not a union.

Safety Is Not the Absence of Conflict, It Is the Presence of Covering

Safety in marriage does not mean you will never fight. It means you will never fear abandonment, humiliation, retaliation, or emotional violence when you do fight.

Safety sounds like:
"You can be honest with me, even when it hurts."
"I will listen without punishing you for speaking."
"We can disagree without threatening the relationship."
"You don't have to disappear to stay connected."

Safety tells the nervous system:
"You can rest here."

And where rest is restored, clarity returns.
Where clarity returns, healing becomes possible.

How Safety Is Actually Rebuilt

Safety is not rebuilt through promises alone. It is rebuilt through a new pattern of response over time. Suspicion does not dissolve in a conversation. It dissolves through consistency.

Safety is rebuilt when:
- Honest words are met with composure instead of explosion
- Vulnerability is met with empathy instead of logic
- Failure is met with correction instead of condemnation
- Struggle is met with partnership instead of pressure

Safety is restored when the heart learns that truth no longer leads to punishment.

Why God Must Be In the Middle of This Process

No couple can rebuild safety through willpower alone. When fear has ruled for a long time, both hearts are tired. Both nervous systems are defensive. Both sides are wounded.

This is where God's presence becomes essential, not as a referee, but as a healer. When Christ enters the fractures, He does not take sides. He restores sight. He softens what has become rigid. He speaks where communication has died.

He does not merely repair conversation.
He heals perception.

The Marriage That Feels Unsafe Is Not Hopeless

Many couples believe the loss of safety is the end. In truth, it is often the beginning of the most honest season they will ever face, if they choose healing instead of hiding.

The loss of safety exposes what never healed beneath the surface.
It reveals what was never spoken.
It surfaces what was only managed.

What is uncovered can be restored.
What is hidden only decays.

From Self-Defense to Shared Defense

Healthy marriage is not two people defending themselves from each other. It is two people defending the union together. Safety is not achieved when one person finally wins. Safety is achieved when both lay down the need to win in order to protect what they are building.

When safety returns, truth returns.
When truth returns, intimacy returns.
When intimacy returns, friendship returns.
And when friendship returns, marriage begins to breathe again.

CHAPTER 9
MONEY PROBLEMS OR PARTNERING PROBLEMS?

The Argument Everyone Thinks Is About Money

Few topics ignite conflict in marriage as quickly as money. It feels practical, measurable, and urgent. Bills are due. Accounts are low. Desires are unmet. Pressure is real. So when tension rises, couples usually conclude, "We have a money problem."

But in many marriages, the greatest issue is not a lack of provision, it is a fracture in partnership.

Money simply becomes the stage where deeper fears, control issues, wounds from the past, and misaligned values finally speak out loud. What appears to be a financial disagreement is often an emotional battle over trust, safety, vision, and leadership.

When partnership weakens, money becomes loud.

How Fear Begins to Write the Budget

Every person carries a financial story long before they carry a paycheck. Some were raised in scarcity. Others were raised in excess. Some watched parents fight constantly over money. Others watched it be avoided entirely. Some were taught to save out of fear. Others were taught to spend out of insecurity.

These experiences quietly shape how we relate to money in adulthood. For one spouse, spending may feel like survival. For another, saving may feel like safety. For one, giving feels like obedience. For another, giving feels like loss.

So when two people marry, they do not just merge bank accounts, they merge financial nervous systems. And when pressure comes, those systems respond exactly as they were trained.

This is why financial conflict often feels irrational. It is not just about numbers. It is about fear trying to protect itself.

Control Masquerading as Wisdom

In many marriages, one spouse quietly assumes the role of financial controller. Sometimes this grows out of genuine skill and wisdom. Other times, it grows out of unresolved anxiety. Control can feel like responsibility when fear is driving the wheel. Statements like, "I'm just being responsible," "I'm just trying to protect us," or "I'm just being realistic," may all be true on the surface, but they can also mask deeper issues of distrust, insecurity, or the subconscious need to regulate outcomes in order to feel safe.

When control replaces collaboration, partnership begins to erode. The budget slowly becomes a battleground. Every purchase starts to feel like a provocation. Every financial decision becomes a referendum on trust rather than a shared act of stewardship. Money, at that point, no longer functions as a tool for building a life together, it becomes a test. And when money becomes a test, fear replaces faith, and suspicion begins to suffocate unity.

When Provision Becomes Personal Worth

For many men, financial provision is silently tied to identity. Success feels like significance. Shortage feels like failure. And when provision is threatened, the fear is not just about bills, it is about worth.

This is why some men grow distant, defensive, or irritable when finances are stressed. They are not just wrestling with math. They are wrestling with meaning.

For many women, financial instability threatens security. It awakens fears of abandonment, uncertainty, and vulnerability. And when safety feels threatened, urgency intensifies. The desire for clarity, structure, and reassurance grows louder.

Both are responding to fear.
Both believe they are protecting the marriage.
But without partnership, both end up fighting each other instead.

Why "My Money" Is a Symptom, Not a Standard

When couples begin to separate finances psychologically, even if accounts remain joined, something sacred begins to fracture. Phrases like "my money," "your money," "my paycheck," and "your spending" reveal more than budgeting issues. They reveal a withdrawal from oneness.

Covenant does not mean reckless spending.
But it does mean shared stewardship.

Money was never meant to be wielded as leverage, withheld as punishment, or used to measure dominance. When it becomes a weapon, partnership has already been wounded.

The Deeper Question Behind Every Financial Argument

Most money arguments are really asking the same questions in different forms:

"Can I trust you?"
"Will you protect me?"
"Do you see me?"
"Are we in this together?"
"Am I alone in the pressure?"

When these questions remain unanswered, the arguments grow louder. Numbers become emotional. Spreadsheets become relational. Decisions become deeply personal.

Money is rarely the root.
It is usually the revealer.

Partnership Changes the Sound of Provision

When partnership is healthy, money begins to speak differently in the home. Pressure still exists. Choices still require wisdom. Sacrifice is still required. But the tone shifts from accusation to agreement. Instead of, "You always spend too much," the language becomes, "How do we navigate this together?" Instead of, "You never give enough," it becomes, "What is God calling us to steward right now?" Instead of, "This is your fault," it becomes, "This is our responsibility." Partnership does not remove financial storms, but it teaches a couple how to face the storm side by side instead of face to face. And when adversity is faced together, it stops being a wedge and becomes a witness to unity.

When God Is Only Invited in After the Panic

Many couples pray about money only when fear has already taken over. They seek God as a rescuer after decisions are already made.

They ask for miracles instead of direction. They plead for provision instead of alignment.

But biblical stewardship begins before the crisis, not after it.

When God is positioned at the center of partnership, money becomes a servant instead of a master. Fear no longer governs decisions. Obedience replaces anxiety. Direction begins to lead what desperation once drove.

The Myth of "If We Just Had More"

Many couples believe their conflict would disappear if their income increased. But money does not heal what misalignment created. It only disguises it.

Abundance does not heal fear.
It often amplifies it.

If partnership is fractured in lack, it usually fractures in abundance as well, just with higher numbers. Without unity, more money simply adds more complexity, more temptation, and more places for conflict to hide.

Money does not solve marital fractures.
It exposes them.

Financial Oneness Is Built, Not Assumed

Oneness in finances does not happen simply because two people are married. It is built through conversation, patience, repentance, compromise, trust, and common vision. It requires each spouse to lay down the need to be right in order to be united.

It requires humility to say:
"I am afraid."
"I don't know."
"I need help."
"I was raised differently."
"I made this decision without you."
"I'm sorry."

These words do more to stabilize a financial future than any budget ever could.

From Survival to Stewardship

When money is governed by fear, couples live in survival mode. Every decision feels urgent, every expense feels threatening, and every shortfall feels catastrophic. Survival constantly asks, "How do we get through this?" But when money is governed by partnership, couples step into stewardship. Stewardship asks a very different question: "What has God entrusted to us, and how do we honor Him together with what we've been given?" Survival hoards, but stewardship releases. Survival reacts impulsively, but stewardship plans with intention. Survival isolates, but stewardship unites. One posture is driven by anxiety and scarcity, while the other is shaped by trust, purpose, and shared responsibility. And the difference between the two is not income, it is alignment.

The Real Healing of Financial Conflict

Financial peace does not come from perfect math. It comes from restored trust. It comes from clear mission. It comes from shared vision. It comes from humility in decision-making. And above all, it comes from the return of partnership under God.

They Shall Be One

When two people truly stand together, money returns to its rightful place: a tool for building, not a test of loyalty.

CHAPTER 10
WHEN DIFFERENCES BECOME "IRRECONCILABLE"

The Differences Were Always There

Most marriages do not break because something suddenly appears. They break because something that always existed finally becomes unbearable. The personalities were always different. The temperaments were always distinct. The weaknesses were always present. The ways of thinking, responding, spending, processing, and communicating were visible from the beginning.

What changes is not the difference. What changes is the value assigned to the difference.

In the early days, difference feels fascinating. It feels complementing. It feels exciting. But when disappointment accumulates and wounds go unattended, those same differences begin to feel threatening. What once felt intriguing now feels intolerable. What once felt balancing now feels opposing. What once felt enriching now feels exhausting.

This is where the phrase "irreconcilable differences" is born. But in most cases, the differences were never truly irreconcilable. What became irreconcilable was the loss of honor.

How Honor Quietly Leaves the Marriage

Honor rarely exits a marriage loudly. It leaves through small dismissals, repeated misunderstandings, unacknowledged effort, unexpressed appreciation, and unresolved resentment. It leaves when one spouse begins to feel unseen. It leaves when one begins to feel taken for granted. It leaves when wounds are minimized and sacrifices go unnoticed.

Over time, admiration fades. Respect thins. Tenderness shrinks. And once honor weakens, difference becomes dangerous.

Without honor, every disagreement feels like disrespect.
Without honor, every conflict feels personal.
Without honor, every flaw feels intentional.

At that point, disagreement is no longer about the issue. It becomes about identity and worth.

Emotional Divorce Before Physical Separation

Many couples emotionally divorce long before they physically separate. They still share a house, a bed, a schedule, and sometimes even laughter, but the heart has withdrawn. They no longer confide. They no longer trust. They no longer expect to be understood.

They begin living parallel lives under the same roof.

This kind of emotional distance is often more painful than open conflict. At least conflict confirms that connection still matters. Silence suggests that hope itself is in danger.

Difference Becomes a Weapon Instead of a Gift

Difference was never meant to divide; it was meant to complement. God designed marriage with contrast on purpose. Strength is meant to meet sensitivity. Stability is meant to meet creativity. Logic is meant to meet intuition. Force is meant to meet finesse. In a healthy marriage, these differences function as gifts that enlarge perspective and deepen balance. One spouse helps the other see what they would otherwise miss. One softens where the other is rigid. One grounds where the other dreams.

But when resentment grows and safety erodes, those same God-designed differences are slowly reinterpreted as defects. What once sounded like, "You help me see what I miss," turns into, "You always see everything wrong." What once felt like, "You soften me," becomes, "You're too emotional." What once was received as, "You ground me," becomes, "You're cold and distant." And in that shift, difference stops being a gift and begins to feel like a grievance. What was meant to mature the marriage is now weaponized to wound it, until redemption restores perspective and honor teaches the heart how to see again.

Why We Fight Hardest Over What Once Attracted Us

One of the great paradoxes of marriage is that people often fight hardest over the very traits that once drew them together. The bold one feels threatening. The cautious one feels suffocating. The dreamer feels irresponsible. The realist feels limiting.

This is not because attraction was wrong.
It is because wounds have rewritten interpretation.

Once fear replaces trust, every trait is filtered through suspicion instead of appreciation. The same behavior no longer feels complementary, it feels confrontational.

When "I'm Done" Is Really "I'm Depleted"

Many times when someone says, "I'm done," what they really mean is "I'm exhausted." They are not rejecting their spouse as much as they are rejecting the relentless emotional strain they no longer know how to navigate.

They are tired of trying.
Tired of explaining.
Tired of hoping.
Tired of being misunderstood.
Tired of feeling alone in the effort.

"I'm done" often masks a heart that once cared deeply, but no longer knows how to endure.

The Slow Death of Curiosity

Healthy marriage is sustained by curiosity:
"Help me understand you."
"What do you feel right now?"
"Why does this matter so much to you?"

But resentment kills curiosity. Once people stop seeking to understand each other, they start seeking to prove each other wrong. Dialogue turns into debate. Listening turns into defense. Understanding turns into winning.

At that point, reconciliation becomes nearly impossible, not because agreement cannot be reached, but because curiosity no longer exists.

Why Some Differences Feel Unforgivable

Some differences carry deeper emotional weight than others. Differences tied to:
- Values
- Faith
- Sexuality

- Parenting
- Loyalty
- Integrity
- Trust

cut closer to the soul. When these areas become battlegrounds, the heart can feel unsafe at the deepest level. And when safety disappears, forgiveness feels impossible, not because grace does not exist, but because the wound never felt protected.

Forgiveness is not difficult because people are cruel.
It is difficult because the pain feels personal and permanent.

Reconciliation Begins With Restored Value, Not Forced Agreement

Most couples try to reconcile by solving the issue. But reconciliation rarely begins with solutions. It begins with restored regard. It begins when two people once again see each other as valuable, even in disagreement.

Healing does not start when you finally agree. It starts when you finally remember why the other person mattered to you.

Without restored honor, compromise feels humiliating.
With restored honor, compromise feels meaningful.

The Question Beneath Every "Irreconcilable" Moment

Beneath every claim of irreconcilable difference lives a deeper question:
"Do you still value me even when you don't understand me?"

When the answer to that question becomes uncertain, difference feels dangerous. But when value is reaffirmed, difference becomes workable again, even when full agreement never arrives.

Differences Do Not End Marriages, Contempt Does

Many couples survive enormous differences. They outlast cultural gaps, family tension, personality contrast, financial strain, and spiritual seasons. What they cannot survive is contempt.

Once one spouse begins to look down on the other, once sarcasm replaces respect, once mockery replaces mercy, and once disgust replaces grace, the foundation begins to crumble.

Scripture warns us that death and life are in the power of the tongue. In marriage, that truth reveals itself with terrifying clarity.

How Hope Begins to Return

Hope does not return when all differences disappear. It returns when the heart softens again. It returns when repentance becomes possible. It returns when humility replaces hostility. It returns when two people are once again willing to say, "Help me understand you," instead of, "You'll never change."

Where softened hearts reappear, reconciliation becomes possible.

From Irreconcilable to Redeemable

Many differences that feel irreconcilable today will feel redemptive tomorrow, if honor can be restored. What once seemed like permanent division can become the very place where maturity is forged, humility is learned, and grace becomes real.

The goal is not uniformity.

They Shall Be One

The goal is unity.

Unity does not require sameness.
It requires shared surrender to something higher than the self.

CHAPTER 11
LOVE, CHOICE, AND THE MYTH OF "FALLING OUT"

The Sentence That Ends Many Marriages

Few phrases carry more power to dissolve a marriage than the words, "I just don't love you anymore." It sounds honest. It sounds final. It sounds emotionally conclusive. And yet, in most cases, it is not a statement about love at all. It is a statement about exhaustion, disappointment, disillusionment, and unhealed pain.

People do not wake up one day and simply lose the capacity to love. They become tired of hurting. They become weary of hoping. They become discouraged by cycles that never seem to change. And slowly, protection replaces pursuit. Numbness replaces desire. Distance replaces devotion.

What leaves first is not love.
What leaves first is the will to keep choosing it.

When We Ask God for Love Instead of Choosing It

One of the most common spiritual deflections in marriage sounds like this: "I've asked God to give me love for them, but He hasn't." That sentence feels humble. It sounds dependent. But often, it quietly shifts responsibility away from the heart and places it on God.

If God commands us to love our enemies, then He has clearly already given us the capacity to love our spouse. The issue is not that love is missing. The issue is that choice has retreated behind disappointment.

Love is not first a feeling.
Love is first a decision to value.

Feelings may follow that decision.
But they rarely lead it.

Why We Confuse Love With Emotion

Modern culture has trained us to define love almost entirely through sensation. Love is portrayed as chemistry, desire, exhilaration, emotional intoxication, and relational electricity. In this framework, when the sensation fades, people assume the substance has vanished with it. When the feelings cool, they believe the love itself has died. But biblical love was never built on intoxication, it was built on covenant.

Covenant does not ask, "How do I feel today?" Covenant asks, "Who did I pledge myself to become for this person?" Emotion is real. Desire is real. Attraction is real. These are God-given dimensions of relationship. But none of them were ever designed to function as the governing authority of marriage. When emotion becomes the ruler, love becomes seasonal and commitment becomes provisional. But when covenant governs, love gains roots that grow deeper than mood, stronger than conflict, and steadier than circumstance.

The Slow Shift From Valuing to Measuring

In the early days of a relationship, people give generously without keeping score. They overlook flaws easily. They extend grace instinctively. They celebrate effort even when it is imperfect. But as wounds accumulate and expectations go unmet, something begins to change internally.

Instead of asking, "How can I bless you?"
People begin asking, "What am I getting back?"

This quiet shift from valuing to measuring is one of the most dangerous transitions in marriage. Once measurement replaces devotion, comparison enters. When comparison enters, resentment follows. And when resentment grows, love begins to feel conditional.

Love was not lost.
It was buried under calculation.

Why Feelings Often Die After Trust Is Wounded

One of the real reasons people say they have "fallen out of love" is because trust has died, not affection. Trust dies through betrayal, abandonment in vulnerability, repeated emotional injury, broken promises, or relational neglect. Once trust collapses, the nervous system goes into protection mode.

Desire cannot thrive where the heart is guarding itself.
Affection cannot flow where the soul feels exposed.
Tenderness cannot grow where the mind expects injury.

So when people say they no longer feel in love, what they are often saying is: "I no longer feel safe."

The Lie of Effortless Love

Another destructive myth is the idea that real love should be effortless. That if it is truly right, it should always feel natural, easy, organic, and spontaneous. This belief makes effort feel like failure and endurance feel like error.

But nothing holy that bears generational weight is effortless.

Faith is not effortless.
Forgiveness is not effortless.
Growth is not effortless.
Healing is not effortless.
Parenting is not effortless.

And marriage is no exception.

Effort does not mean love is dying.
Effort means love is maturing.

The Moment Love Becomes a Daily Choice

There is a sacred moment in every lasting marriage when love transitions from something you feel to someone you choose. This is the moment when romance becomes covenant. When emotion becomes devotion. When desire becomes discipline.

This is not the loss of love.
This is the deepening of it.

This is where love becomes conscious.
This is where sacrifice gains meaning.
This is where maturity replaces fantasy.

And this is where many people turn back, because they confuse the end of intoxication with the end of love.

Why People "Fall Out" When They Expected to Be Carried

Some people marry expecting love to carry them forever. They expect the relationship to sustain them without sustained effort. They expect affection to compensate for character gaps. They expect chemistry to overcome incompatibility. They expect feelings to conquer formation.

But marriage was never designed to carry people.
It was designed to shape them.

When love is treated as a source instead of a stewarded fire, disappointment is inevitable. Love must be tended. It must be protected. It must be guarded from contempt. It must be chosen daily in the face of inconvenience.

Fire that is not tended does not disappear instantly.
It slowly dims.

Choosing to Love When It No Longer Feels Natural

One of the most powerful spiritual acts in marriage is choosing love when emotion grows quiet. This is where covenant is purified. This is where motive is tested. This is where grace becomes real. Choosing love in these moments does not look dramatic, it looks faithful. It looks like listening when you would rather withdraw, forgiving when pride wants revenge, staying present when escape feels easier, honoring when disappointment feels justified, and serving even when nothing appears to be returned. This is not weakness. This is Christlikeness. This is love stripped of performance and anchored in promise.

Love Does Not Die, It Is Either Fed or Starved

Love does not mysteriously vanish. It is either nourished or neglected. It grows where appreciation lives, and it withers where contempt is allowed to rule. It strengthens where humility survives, and it fades where pride dominates. Love itself is not fragile, it is responsive. Where value is restored, love often reawakens. Where honor returns, affection frequently follows. And where safety is patiently rebuilt, desire often finds its way back as well.

This is why the real question beneath "Do I still love you?" is rarely about emotion at all. The deeper question is almost always this: Am I still willing to choose you in this season of pressure, disappointment, and imperfection? Covenant does not ask whether love feels easy. Covenant asks whether love is still willing. And that willingness, quiet, steady, and determined, is where the power of covenant truly lives.

Love as an Act of Worship

At its deepest level, choosing to love your spouse is not just a relational decision, it is a spiritual one. It is not only devotion to a person; it is obedience to a calling. It is service rendered not only to a spouse, but to God Himself.

Love becomes an act of worship when:
You choose it without applause.
You sustain it without recognition.
You extend it without guarantee.
You protect it without reward.

This is where marriage stops being about personal fulfillment alone and becomes a reflection of Christ and the Church once again.

From "Fallen Out" to "Fully Chosen"

Many who believe they have fallen out of love have not lost love at all. They have simply reached the place where love requires conscious choice instead of emotional momentum. And that place, though uncomfortable, is where the truest form of love is born.

Not the kind that thrills for a moment.
But the kind that endures for a lifetime.

CHAPTER 12
ROMANCE, COVENANT, AND THE WAR BETWEEN FEELING AND FAITHFULNESS

When Romance Becomes the Measurement of Love

Modern culture has trained us to measure love almost entirely through romance. Music, movies, social media, and storytelling have taught us that love is proven by sensation, by chemistry, by spark, by emotional electricity, by how intensely someone makes us feel. In this framework, love is not something we steward. It is something that either happens to us or fades from us.

This is why so many people panic when the early intensity of romance begins to settle. They interpret the quieting of emotional adrenaline as a warning sign rather than a natural transition. They conclude something is wrong when, in reality, something is simply changing form.

Romance was never meant to be the foundation of marriage. It was meant to be a gift of marriage. When it becomes the foundation, the structure is built on sensation instead of covenant. And sensations, by their very nature, fluctuate.

Why Culture Prefers Romance Over Covenant

Romance feels powerful because it requires no discipline. It rises without training, ignites without effort, surges without responsibility. Covenant, on the other hand, requires endurance. It demands consistency. It calls for sacrifice. It insists on maturity.

Romance makes us feel alive, but covenant teaches us how to live faithfully. One stirs emotion; the other forges character.

Our culture celebrates what excites us but avoids what forms us. It elevates passion but minimizes perseverance. It honors thrill while resisting transformation. This is why romance is glamorized while covenant is often treated as restrictive. Yet covenant is not restriction, it is construction. It does not suffocate love; it shelters it. Covenant builds what romance alone can never sustain, because romance can ignite a relationship, but only covenant can carry it through fire, through pressure, through change, and through time.

When Feelings Become a Tyrant

Feelings are powerful but they were never meant to be sovereign. When emotion becomes the governing authority of a marriage, it begins to tyrannize decision-making. People no longer ask, "What is right?" They ask, "What feels right?" They no longer ask, "What is faithful?" They ask, "What is fulfilling right now?"

This shift has enormous consequences.

When feeling governs:
- Commitment becomes negotiable
- Sacrifice becomes optional
- Endurance becomes foolish
- And obedience becomes conditional

Yet Scripture never commands us to be led by feeling. It repeatedly calls us to be led by faith, truth, and love expressed through obedience.

Feelings make excellent servants.
They make terrible masters.

The Great Deception: That Romance and Covenant Are the Same

Many people unknowingly marry romance expecting it to behave like covenant. They assume the same chemistry that ignited the relationship will also sustain it. But romance and covenant are not the same thing.

Romance says, "I love how you make me feel."
Covenant says, "I commit to who I choose to become for you."

Romance asks, "Do you still thrill me?"
Covenant asks, "Do you still matter to me?"

Romance is reactive.
Covenant is decisive.

When romance fades, as it inevitably does in seasons, those who married romance panic. They assume the relationship has failed, when in truth it has simply entered the season where covenant is required to lead.

Why Affairs Are Often About Feeling, Not Desire

Many extramarital emotional or physical attachments do not begin with lust. They begin with longing to be felt again. Someone laughs at what your spouse no longer hears. Someone notices what has grown invisible at home. Someone affirms what now feels overlooked.

Affairs are rarely just about sex.
They are about sensation replacing stewardship.

The mistake is not the desire to feel again.
The mistake is choosing feeling over faithfulness.

Affairs do not begin because covenant failed.

They begin because covenant was no longer chosen above emotion.

Romance Is a Gift, But It Must Be Protected From Idolatry

God is not against romance. He created desire. He designed attraction. He authored intimacy. The Song of Solomon stands as a witness to the beauty of passion within covenant. But romance is meant to live inside covenant, not replace it.

When romance becomes an idol, it begins to demand sacrifices it was never meant to receive. People sacrifice consistency for excitement. They sacrifice loyalty for novelty. They sacrifice history for hunger. They sacrifice family for feeling.

Whatever we enthrone will eventually demand everything.

Covenant Is What Carries Love Through Seasons

Every marriage passes through seasons, seasons of passion, seasons of pressure, seasons of fatigue, seasons of rebuilding, seasons of quiet, and seasons of renewal. These seasons are not signs of failure; they are simply the rhythm of real life shared between two imperfect people growing together. Romance alone does not carry a marriage through these seasons. Covenant does.

Covenant remains when passion grows quiet. Covenant remains when conflict grows loud. Covenant remains when feelings feel confusing and when hope feels fragile. This is why covenant is not merely emotional, it is architectural. It is the framework that holds the house together when storms strike the structure. Feelings may rise and fall with the season, but covenant remains the load-bearing wall that keeps the marriage standing when everything else is being tested.

Faithfulness Is Love Under Authority

Faithfulness is love submitted to something higher than desire. It is love governed by promise instead of appetite. It is love rooted in identity instead of impulse.

Faithfulness says:
"I will not abandon what my feelings cannot currently affirm."
"I will not rewrite my vows based on my mood."
"I will not trade legacy for momentary relief."

Faithfulness is not the absence of attraction.
It is the presence of discipline.

The Redemption of Romance Through Covenant

One of the great surprises of covenant is that romance often returns more deeply after it has seemingly "died." When two people walk through disappointment without abandoning one another, when they endure difficult seasons without choosing escape, and when they remain present for each other without applause or recognition, something new is quietly born. Not intoxication, but intimacy. Not adrenaline, but attachment. Not fantasy, but friendship.

This kind of romance does not demand, it responds. It is not fueled by illusion or performance, but by survival together. It grows out of storms weathered side by side, out of prayers whispered in uncertainty, out of endurance that refused to quit. It is a romance shaped by reality, strengthened by loyalty, and deepened by shared history. And unlike the romance of fantasy, this kind of love is not fragile. It is forged.

Why Faithfulness Feels Unromantic, But Changes Everything

Faithfulness rarely feels poetic in the moment. It looks like choosing the same person again when nothing feels dramatic. It looks like staying present on ordinary days. It looks like extending grace when no one is watching. It looks like consistency without applause.

Yet faithfulness changes everything over time.

It builds trust.
It builds safety.
It builds legacy.
It builds generational stability.
It builds something romance alone cannot produce.

From Feeling-Driven to Covenant-Governed

When a marriage shifts from being feeling-driven to covenant-governed, peace begins to replace volatility. Stability replaces anxiety. Endurance replaces panic. And freedom replaces fear—not the freedom to leave, but the freedom to rest inside a vow that no longer feels fragile.

This is where love grows up.

Romance Is Beautiful, But Covenant Is Holy

Romance can be intense.
Romance can be thrilling.
Romance can be intoxicating.

But covenant is sacred.

Romance celebrates the moment.

Covenant preserves the future.

Romance feels powerful.
Covenant is powerful.

CHAPTER 13

DID GOD EVER ENTER THE MARRIAGE? RETURNING TO THE BEGINNING FOR HEALING

The Wedding That Consumed the Marriage

For many couples, the greatest investment of time, money, energy, and emotion came not in building the marriage, but in staging the event that introduced it. Engagement becomes a season of pressure. Decisions multiply. Finances strain. Expectations rise. Stress dominates. And by the time the wedding arrives, many couples are already tired, already tense, already in debt, already stretched thin.

The tragedy is not that weddings are celebrated. The tragedy is when the celebration becomes so consuming that the marriage itself becomes an afterthought.

Some couples sense the imbalance and quietly choose a courthouse ceremony, hoping to avoid the weight of expectation. But even then, many carry an unspoken awareness that something important was never fully addressed. Whether through extravagance or simplicity, the same danger remains: the wedding becomes the focus, while the covenant remains undefined.

The result is a culture that trains us to prepare for a day while neglecting a lifetime.

When God Was Honored in the Ceremony but Never Invited into the Decision

Many couples sincerely believe they invited God into their marriage because they prayed on the wedding day, chose worship music, or stood before a minister. Yet honoring God in a ceremony is not the same as seeking God in a decision. A wedding can be spiritual in appearance while the formation of the marriage itself remained largely self-directed. There are couples who genuinely honored God in the celebration but never truly invited Him into the construction of the covenant.

Some married out of loneliness. Some married out of desire. Some married because the timing seemed right. Others married from pressure, family pressure, cultural pressure, or the pressure of expectations. Some married because the relationship had gone too far emotionally, physically, or relationally to turn back. Others married because they believed, "This must be God, it feels right." But feeling is not the same as leading. Emotion can affirm a choice, but it was never designed to author one.

There are many couples who invited God into the celebration, but never truly invited Him into the formation. They asked Him to bless what they had already chosen rather than to lead what they were deciding. And while God is merciful and faithful even in our missteps, alignment always brings a different kind of authority, peace, and endurance into a marriage than momentum ever could.

The Question That Determines the Starting Line

One of the most healing questions a couple can ever ask is not about arguments, finances, trust, or intimacy. It is this:

"Did we ever ask God if this was His will, or did we only ask Him to bless what we had already chosen?"

That question does not condemn.
It clarifies.

Because if God was never truly invited into the beginning, then healing must always return to the origin point.

Why Healing Must Go Backward Before It Can Move Forward

In Scripture, repentance is not merely sorrow. The Greek word used throughout the New Testament is metanoeō (μετανοέω). It means to change the mind, to turn, to reorient the way one thinks. It is not just a confession of wrongdoing, it is a repositioning of direction.

Many couples try to heal by managing symptoms:
Better communication.
Better boundaries.
Better habits.
Better routines.

But some wounds remain stubborn because the fracture was not merely behavioral, it was foundational. The marriage did not begin on revelation. It began on assumption.

And what began without divine alignment often cannot be healed without divine re-entry.

The Power of Inviting God in, Even After Decades

One of the most breathtaking truths of grace is that God does not demand we go back in time to redo our decisions, He allows us to return in heart and begin again with Him right where we are. A couple can be married five years, twenty years, or even fifty years and still say with full sincerity, "Lord, we are inviting You into this marriage now." This is not a denial of history; it is the redemption of it. It is not regret, it is surrender. It is not restarting life, it is restarting alignment.

And when God is invited into a covenant that once moved forward without Him, He does not enter with accusation. He enters with healing. He does not come to shame what was broken; He comes to restore what was wounded. Where misalignment once governed, grace begins to realign. Where fear once shaped decisions, love begins to reframe them. And what once limped forward under human strength alone can begin again under divine covering and restored design.

Asking Forgiveness for Beginning Without Direction

For some couples, one of the most liberating moments in their entire marriage is when they finally say out loud, together, "We did this without You." Not in shame. Not in condemnation. But in truth. And in that truth, something breaks, not the couple, but the weight they have been carrying in silence. When truth is spoken without accusation, it becomes a doorway instead of a verdict.

Forgiveness does not rewrite the wedding, but it does redeem the marriage that followed it. When a couple repents together, they are not confessing failure, they are choosing alignment over pride. They are stepping out of defense and into humility. They are no longer protecting the past; they are surrendering it. And in that surrender, God is given room to heal what honesty has finally uncovered.

The Lie That It's "Too Late"

One of the most destructive lies in marriage is the belief that healing had a window and that window has passed. That because patterns are deep, wounds are old, habits are entrenched, and disappointment is layered, restoration is no longer realistic.

But Scripture never reveals a God who is intimidated by time.

What feels late to us is often simply ready to Him.

God does not measure opportunity by chronology.
He measures it by yielded hearts.

When a Marriage Is Re-dedicated Instead of Just Maintained

There is a difference between maintaining a marriage and re-dedicating it.

Maintenance manages decline.
Rededication invites renewal.

Maintenance keeps the same structure alive.
Rededication allows God to reform the foundation from the inside out.

Some of the most powerful turning points in marriage happen not when everything is falling apart, but when everything has become stale, dutiful, quiet, and distant. The couple is not fighting. They have simply stopped believing anything can be different.

That is often the moment God is waiting for.

The Beginning Is Always Where God Heals

In Scripture, God consistently heals by returning people to beginnings:
He takes Israel back to Abraham.
He takes hearts back to first love.
He takes faith back to promise.
He takes the Church back to Christ.

And in marriage, He takes couples back to why they were joined in the first place. Not to shame them. But to restore the purpose they lost sight of along the way.

Re-Inviting God Is Not a Religious Act, It Is a Relational Surrender

Inviting God into a marriage does not mean adding prayer to dysfunction. It means surrendering the governance of the home. It means no longer asking God to bless decisions, but allowing Him to direct them again.

This is where real healing begins.

Not when behavior improves.
Not when communication gets smoother.
But when Lordship is restored.

The Courage to Begin Again Without Erasing the Past

Some couples hesitate to re-invite God because they fear it will highlight where they failed. But God does not expose the past to condemn it. He exposes it to heal it without erasing its lessons.

He does not require amnesia.
He offers renewal.

And renewal never denies what has been.
It redeems what remains.

The New Beginning That Is Still Possible

Some couples reading this have been married for decades and quietly believe it is too late for a true beginning. But there is no expiration date on surrender. There is no cutoff for restoration.

They Shall Be One

There is no age limit on intimacy. There is no season God cannot redeem.

The question is not:
"How long have we been broken?"

The question is:
"Are we willing to invite God into this now?"

Because the moment a marriage truly returns to Him, no matter how late it feels, the beginning quietly comes again.

CHAPTER 14
COMPATIBLE PURPOSE OR CONVENIENT CHOICE?

When "This Will Do" Replaces "This Was Led"

Not every marriage begins with rebellion. Many begin with fatigue. People grow tired of waiting. Tired of praying. Tired of hoping. Tired of being alone. And somewhere in the quiet weariness of longing, the question silently shifts from "Is this God's will?" to "Will this work?"

At that moment, marriage becomes a convenient choice instead of a compatible purpose.

There is a subtle but profound difference between choosing someone because you are led and choosing someone because you are ready. Readiness does not always mean alignment. Desire does not always mean direction. And loneliness can speak with an urgency that sounds like love but lacks the voice of wisdom.

"This person will do" is one of the most dangerous sentences a soul can whisper to itself.

Passion Without Purpose Always Runs Out of Meaning

Passion can sustain pursuit for a season. Chemistry can carry curiosity. Desire can intensify attachment. But none of these can shoulder the long weight of life. They were never designed to be load-bearing realities.

Purpose is what bears weight.

When a marriage is built on passion without purpose, it often begins with intense energy and ends in profound confusion. The couple loves each other, but they do not know why they are together beyond feeling. And when feeling softens, as it inevitably does under pressure, the relationship begins to drift.

Passion asks, "How do you make me feel?"
Purpose asks, "What are we called to build together?"

Without that second question being clearly answered, marriage becomes an emotional experience instead of a generational assignment.

Why Love Alone Is Not a Sufficient Foundation

Love is essential. It is holy. It is powerful. But love alone, without vision, direction, and shared purpose, is not a foundation, it is a fuel. And fuel without direction burns wildly and aimlessly.

Many couples genuinely love each other and still drift into resentment. Not because their love was false, but because their lives were never aimed in the same direction. They were walking side-by-side emotionally, but they were not traveling toward the same destination spiritually.

Love can unite hearts.
Only purpose can unite futures.

When Compatibility Is Measured Only by Preference

Modern compatibility is often measured by surface harmony: shared hobbies, similar tastes, aligned personalities, mutual attraction, and emotional resonance. These things matter, but they are insufficient for covenant.

True compatibility is not first about preference.
It is about direction.

Two people can enjoy the same music, laugh at the same jokes, and love the same foods, and still be covenant-misaligned. Enjoyment does not equal direction. Agreement does not equal assignment.

The question is not only:
"Do we like the same things?"

The deeper question is:
"Are we moving toward the same God-defined outcome?"

The Subtle Tragedy of Directionless Devotion

One of the quietest tragedies in marriage is the couple who is deeply devoted to each other, but drifting aimlessly through life together. They are loyal. They are faithful. They are affectionate. But they do not feel fulfilled. Something always feels missing.

They cannot name it.
They just feel it.

That ache is often the absence of shared calling. Devotion without direction eventually feels like sacrifice without meaning. And sacrifice without meaning always breeds frustration.

When Attraction Chooses Before Wisdom Speaks

Attraction is powerful because it speaks instantly. Wisdom speaks slowly. Attraction speaks to the body. Wisdom speaks to the future. Attraction feels urgent. Wisdom feels patient.

Many couples marry in the moment where attraction is loud and wisdom is still whispering. Later, when wisdom finally finds its voice, it often sounds like regret, confusion, or disillusionment, not because the person was wrong, but because the process was bypassed.

Attraction is not evil.
But attraction without discernment is dangerous.

Why Purpose Clarifies What Love Alone Confuses

Purpose does something miraculous in marriage, it interprets pain. When a couple truly knows why they are together, suffering no longer feels random. Sacrifice no longer feels wasted. Delay no longer feels punishing. Purpose does not remove hardship, but it gives hardship meaning. It places pain inside a larger story so that pressure no longer feels pointless.

Without purpose, struggle feels like loss. Delay feels like injustice. Sacrifice feels like exploitation. But with purpose, everything is reframed. Struggle becomes training. Delay becomes preparation. Sacrifice becomes investment. What once felt like something being taken away now begins to feel like something being built. Purpose transforms endurance from mere survival into intentional formation, and that transformation changes the emotional atmosphere of the entire marriage.

When One Wakes Up and the Other Still Sleeps

Some marriages experience a powerful shift when one spouse awakens to purpose while the other remains comfortably settled in convenience. One begins asking deeper questions about calling, direction, impact, and legacy. The other is content with routine, predictability, and emotional stability alone.

This creates tension, not because one is sinful and the other is holy, but because movement has become asymmetrical. One is stepping into calling. The other is standing in comfort.

If this tension is not navigated with humility and communication, it can easily turn into accusation, superiority, or spiritual isolation. But if it is navigated in prayer and partnership, it can become the very mechanism God uses to awaken both hearts.

Why Some Marriages Feel Like Resistance Instead of Reinforcement

Marriage was designed to be a place of reinforcement—where calling is strengthened, courage is multiplied, and obedience is supported. But when purpose is misaligned, marriage can begin to feel like resistance instead of reinforcement.

Instead of pushing each other forward, couples begin to unconsciously pull each other backward—not through manipulation, but through fear, misunderstanding, or unresolved insecurity.

This is one of the most painful tensions in marriage:
To love someone deeply and still feel unreinforced in your becoming.

Convenient Choice Always Avoids the Cost of Calling

Calling always carries a cost, while convenience is designed to avoid one. Calling demands courage; convenience demands comfort. Calling requires obedience; convenience prefers ease. When marriage is chosen for convenience rather than calling, the cost of obedience eventually shows up anyway, but without the grace that calling supplies. The price is still paid. The sacrifice still arrives. The pressure still comes. The only difference is that the couple now bears the weight without understanding the meaning behind it. And when cost is endured without calling, suffering feels confusing instead of purposeful, and endurance feels heavy instead of holy.

Healing the Marriage That Began as a Convenient Choice

Not every marriage began with clarity of purpose. Many began in confusion, desire, pressure, insecurity, or timing. But the mercy of God is that purpose can still be revealed after the fact.

God is not limited by how something began.
He is only limited by whether we will let Him re-direct it.

A marriage that began in convenience can be re-anchored in calling. A relationship formed in emotion can be re-established in mission. A covenant entered blindly can still be illuminated by revelation. Compatible purpose is not only something you discern before marriage. It is something you can still discover within it.

From "Will This Work?" to "Why Were We Joined?"

The most important shift a couple can make is from asking:
"Will this work?"
to asking:
"Why were we joined?"

One question is rooted in survival.
The other is rooted in destiny.

And destiny always reorders everything.

CHAPTER 15

LOVING WHO THEY WILL BECOME, NOT JUST WHO THEY ARE

The Version of Them You Married Is Not the Version God Is Finished With

Every couple marries a version, not a finished work. We marry people in process, even when we speak vows as if the person standing before us is the final outcome. Yet Scripture is unambiguous about this truth: God is always at work shaping, healing, revealing, delivering, maturing, and transforming His people. Marriage does not pause that work. It places transformation under the brightest possible light.

This is why one of the great hidden tests of covenant is not whether we can love who our spouse is, it is whether we can love who God is making them to be.

Many couples celebrate change in theory but resist it in practice. We pray for healing until healing begins to disrupt dependency. We pray for leadership until leadership challenges control. We pray for confidence until confidence removes leverage. We pray for freedom until freedom threatens familiar power dynamics.

Growth is wonderful, unless it costs us something.

When Healing Threatens the Old Arrangement

Some wives marry men who are insecure, withdrawn, passive, or deeply wounded, and over time they quietly become strong in order to compensate. They organize life. They manage emotions. They make decisions. They stabilize chaos. At first, this strength feels necessary. Eventually, it becomes normal. The marriage adapts around her capacity to hold everything together.

Then God begins to heal the man. He finds his voice. He becomes decisive. He grows in spiritual authority. He steps into responsibility. And suddenly, what the wife once prayed for no longer feels comfortable, because now she must relinquish a role she learned to survive in. What once felt necessary now feels risky. A strength that was forged in survival is now being asked to surrender to partnership, and that transition can feel terrifying even when it is healthy.

Likewise, some men marry women who are emotionally dependent, fearful, unsure, or fragile. The man becomes the emotional anchor, the provider of certainty, the source of stability. Over time, that dependency can subtly become a source of identity and even power. Being needed begins to feel like being valued.

Then God begins to heal the woman. She finds her confidence. She gains clarity. She grows spiritually. She becomes internally stable. And suddenly, what the man once felt needed now feels threatening, because his role as rescuer is no longer required in the same way. The ground shifts beneath the identity he unconsciously built around being indispensable.

In both of these stories, healing is not the problem. Insecurity is. Healing exposes what survival once hid. It challenges roles that were formed out of necessity instead of design. But true restoration does not dismantle marriage, it redeems it. It does not erase strength; it relocates it into shared leadership. And when insecurity is brought into the light, partnership finally has space to emerge where compensation once ruled.

The Fear Beneath Resistance to Change

Resistance to a spouse's growth is rarely about theology. It is almost always about fear. Fear of becoming unnecessary. Fear of losing influence. Fear of being left behind. Fear of being exposed. Fear of losing control. When transformation begins in one spouse, it often reveals unresolved identity struggles in the other. Instead of celebrating the growth they once prayed for, the threatened spouse may respond with suspicion, criticism, withdrawal, or even accusation.

They may never say out loud, "I'm afraid I'm losing my place." Instead, they say things like, "You've changed," or, "You're not the same anymore," or, "That's not who I married." And in one sense, that is true. They are not the same. That is the point. Growth, by its very nature, means change. Healing means transformation. Maturity means evolution. The tragedy is not that someone changes, it is when change is treated as betrayal instead of breakthrough.

Why Some Marriages Break During the Best Season of Change

It is one of the great paradoxes of marriage that some relationships rupture not in seasons of sin, but in seasons of healing. The addiction is confronted. The trauma is addressed. The emotional wounds are being repaired. The person is becoming whole.

And the marriage collapses.

Not because healing failed, but because the relationship was silently built on dysfunction as a stabilizing force. When dysfunction leaves, the structure that adapted to it collapses unless the covenant evolves with the transformation.

In other words, some marriages were not bound together by health.

They were bound together by what both people learned to survive.

When survival is no longer required, the marriage must learn how to exist in freedom instead of fear.

Loving the Becoming Requires Humility, Not Control

To love who someone will become requires extraordinary humility. It requires the willingness to admit that you do not own your spouse's future. It requires the surrender of scripts you quietly wrote for their life. It requires the laying down of old power arrangements that once felt necessary.

Covenant love does not say, "Stay who you are so I can stay comfortable."

Covenant love says, "Become all God designed you to be, even if it costs me something."

This does not mean abandoning structure or order. It means allowing growth without retaliation and transformation without threat.

When Growth Exposes Unequal Development

Some tension in marriage arises because growth does not always happen symmetrically. One spouse may awaken spiritually, emotionally, or professionally long before the other. One begins asking deeper questions. The other is still content with the status quo.

This uneven development can feel deeply unsettling. The one who is growing may feel lonely, misunderstood, or restrained. The one who is not growing may feel judged, inadequate, or left behind.

If this season is not navigated with grace, it can quickly turn into resentment on both sides. The growing spouse feels unsupported. The stationary spouse feels condemned. And what began as personal transformation becomes relational pressure.

The goal is not for both to grow at the same speed.
The goal is for both to honor the process the other is in.

The Difference Between Growth and Abandonment

Some resist their spouse's growth because they confuse change with departure. They fear that transformation means replacement. They assume that if their spouse becomes stronger, freer, wiser, or more spiritually alive, they will eventually outgrow the relationship itself.

But growth does not automatically mean abandonment.
It only means abandonment when covenant is no longer valued.

Growth under covenant says, "I am becoming more, and I am bringing that 'more' back into our union."

Growth without covenant says, "I am becoming more, and I no longer need you."

The difference is not growth.
The difference is the heart's loyalty.

The Marriage Must Evolve If the People Do

Every living thing must grow or it stagnates. Marriage is no different. A covenant that refuses to evolve becomes brittle. It survives only by suppressing development instead of stewarding it.

Healthy marriage does not freeze people in the season they were married.

It learns how to love them through every season they become.

The student becomes the teacher.
The struggler becomes the leader.
The wounded becomes the healer.
The insecure becomes the stable.

And with every transition, the covenant must stretch.

Why God Intentionally Allows Discomfort in Growth

Discomfort is not the sign that something is wrong. Often, it is the sign that something is being reformed. God allows discomfort because it exposes what we attached to for safety instead of surrendering to Him.

Growth reveals:

Where identity was borrowed.
Where dependency replaced faith.
Where control masked insecurity.
Where comfort replaced obedience.

These exposures are not meant to shame.
They are meant to free.

Loving Without Trying to Freeze

True covenant love refuses to freeze a person in the version of themselves that made us feel most secure. It refuses to trap someone in who they were when we met. It refuses to idolize the past at the expense of God's future.

Love says:
"I will not demand that you remain small so I can remain powerful."

"I will not resist your healing because it changes our arrangement."
"I will not punish your growth because it exposes my wounds."

This kind of love is not indulgent.
It is cruciform.

Becoming Together Without Becoming Enemies

The goal of marriage is not for one to become while the other resists. It is for both to become together, even when the timing differs. It is for conversation to remain open, prayer to remain shared, and curiosity to remain alive.

When couples talk about growth instead of hiding it, when they invite each other into the process instead of threatening with it, transformation becomes mutual instead of divisive.

Covenant Is Not Frozen Agreement, It Is Living Alignment

Covenant is not a signed document that never moves. It is living alignment under a living God. As God speaks, leads, heals, and redirects, covenant must remain responsive rather than rigid.

To love who your spouse will become is to trust not only them, but the God who is forming them.

The Hidden Question Each Spouse Must Face

Beneath every season of transformation, each spouse faces the same hidden question:

"Will I love you only when your change benefits me, or will I love you even when your change challenges me?"

Christopher K. Turney

The answer to that question reveals the true condition of covenant.

CHAPTER 16
WHEN SUBMISSION BECOMES A THREAT INSTEAD OF A TRUST

The Moment Submission Stops Feeling Safe

Submission was designed to be the response of trust, not the reflex of fear. Yet for many, the word itself now carries tension, defensiveness, and even dread. This is not because the biblical design is flawed. It is because the relational environment meant to support submission has often been broken.

Submission only functions where trust is alive. The moment trust erodes, submission begins to feel like vulnerability without protection. It no longer feels like alignment, it feels like exposure. And once exposure feels dangerous, the heart instinctively resists.

This is why many spouses do not reject the idea of order, they reject the risk of being unprotected inside it.

Trust Is the Currency That Makes Submission Possible

No one can submit where they do not trust. Trust is not built through command; it is built through consistency. It is formed through truth, accountability, humility, and visible integrity lived out over time. Trust grows when words and actions repeatedly agree, when repentance is real, when responsibility is owned, and when love is demonstrated rather than declared. Submission that flows from this kind of trust does not feel like loss, it feels like safety.

When trust is present, submission sounds like, "I am safe to follow you." It feels like, "I trust your heart." It rests in the confidence that says, "I believe your direction includes my good." But when trust is absent, submission feels dangerous. It feels like, "I will be exposed," or, "I may be overrun," or, "I will lose myself here." One environment invites peace. The other awakens self-defense. And where self-defense rules, covenant cannot breathe freely, but where trust lives, alignment becomes a refuge rather than a risk.

How Control Enters When Safety Leaves

When submission feels unsafe, control often rises as a substitute for protection. Control is not always driven by rebellion. Many times, it is driven by fear that no one else is truly guarding the direction of the home.

Control says:
"If I don't manage this, everything will collapse."
"If I don't decide this, no one will."
"If I don't correct this, it will never change."

While it may look domineering on the outside, it is often rooted in a deep sense of vulnerability underneath.

Control is what fear uses to simulate safety.

Why Some Men Fear Submission as Much as Some Women

Submission does not only feel threatening to women, it feels threatening to men too, though for different reasons. Some men fear submission because they associate it with weakness rather than alignment. They equate yielding with losing authority instead of stewarding it.

Yet biblical submission does not flow in only one direction, it flows upward and inward under God's order. The man submits to Christ. The woman submits to God's order through the man. And together, both submit to the Lordship of Christ as one. This is not a hierarchy of value; it is a sequence of alignment. No one stands independent. No one governs autonomously. Each life is anchored to Christ first, and then joined to one another through Him.

Submission, therefore, is not gendered weakness. It is relational obedience. It is the shared posture of two people who have chosen to come under divine order rather than human control. It is not about dominance and disappearance, it is about trust and alignment under the authority of Christ. And when submission is restored to this sacred placement, it no longer feels oppressive; it feels protective, ordered, and safe.

When Headship Becomes Pressure Instead of Covering

Headship was never meant to be a burden placed on a woman's shoulders to endure. It was meant to be a covering over her life, not a weight crushing her beneath it. When headship shifts from protection to pressure, the entire design is violated.

Christ does not lead His Church through intimidation. He leads through self-giving love. When leadership in the home no longer resembles Christ, submission begins to feel spiritually unsafe, even if Scripture is being quoted.

The Difference Between Leading and Demanding

Leadership and domination may look similar from a distance, but they produce entirely different atmospheres in a marriage. Leadership invites; domination demands. Leadership takes responsibility for outcomes; domination shifts blame when things go wrong.

Leadership is willing to absorb consequence in order to protect those it serves, while domination inflicts consequence in order to maintain control. Leadership creates safety, but domination manufactures compliance.

This is why biblical submission responds to leadership, but it instinctively resists domination. Submission is drawn toward covering, not coercion. It aligns with responsibility, not intimidation. Where leadership is present, submission feels like trust. Where domination rules, submission feels like threat. One grows covenant. The other erodes it.

When Submission Feels Like Erasure

Some resist submission not because they reject order, but because they fear disappearing inside it. They fear losing their voice, their agency, their discernment, their identity, their strengths, and their sense of self.

True submission never erases identity, it aligns identity. In covenant, you do not become less; you become joined. You do not disappear into another's shadow; you become integrated into shared purpose. Biblical submission does not flatten individuality, it harmonizes it. It brings two distinct lives into ordered unity without deleting the uniqueness of either one.

Where submission erases personhood, it is no longer biblical, it has quietly become control. God never restores order by destroying identity. He restores order by aligning identity under His authority. Anything that requires a person to shrink, silence their conscience, abandon their voice, or forfeit their God-given agency is not submission, it is distortion. In true covenant, identity is not sacrificed on the altar of order; it is secured within it.

Why Unhealed Trauma Distorts Submission

For those who have experienced neglect, abandonment, coercion, abuse, or unseen childhood wounds, submission can trigger deep emotional alarms. What Scripture calls trust, the nervous system may interpret as danger.

In these cases, resistance to submission is not rebellion, it is the body remembering what the soul once survived.

This is why healing is essential.
Not to force submission.
But to restore the capacity to trust again.

Submission Without Safety Is Spiritual Endangerment

No Scripture ever commands a person to submit to what violates God's nature. Abuse, manipulation, intimidation, coercion, and sin were never meant to be supported under the banner of submission.

Submission is alignment with God's mission under God's character.

When character is absent, submission is not spiritual, it is dangerous.

How Submission Is Restored After It Has Been Broken

Restoring submission does not begin with renewed instruction. It begins with renewed safety. Before alignment can return, cover must be demonstrated. Before trust can be rebuilt, humility must be visible.

This happens when leadership:
- Repents without excuse
- Listens without defensiveness
- Protects without controlling

- Leads without posturing
- Serves without expectation

Submission returns naturally where love becomes predictable again.

When Submission Becomes Strength Again

When submission is restored to trust, it becomes one of the most powerful forces in marriage. It no longer feels like loss. It feels like multiplication. It no longer feels like disappearance. It feels like partnership under divine order.

Submission becomes:
A response to safety.
A gift of trust.
A posture of unity.
A movement of faith.

From Threat Back to Trust

Submission does not become a threat overnight. It becomes a threat slowly, when trust is violated, when protection is absent, when accountability disappears, and when fear quietly takes the wheel. What was once meant to feel like covering begins to feel like exposure. What was designed to feel like safety begins to feel like risk. In that environment, submission no longer feels like trust, it feels like surrendering to danger.

But submission becomes trust again when the landscape changes. It is restored when love becomes consistent instead of conditional, when leadership becomes sacrificial instead of self-serving, when truth becomes safe instead of punished, and when God returns to the center of the marriage again. In that atmosphere, submission is no longer something to survive, it becomes something to rest in. Safety revives alignment, and trust once again has room to breathe.

The Question That Determines Everything

At the core of submission is one defining question:
"Do I believe that following here will not lead me away from God, but closer to Him?"

If the answer is yes, submission feels secure.
If the answer is no, resistance feels necessary.

This is why submission can only survive where Christ truly leads.

CHAPTER 17
THE WAR BETWEEN APPRECIATION AND RESENTMENT

The Quiet Battlefield Inside Most Marriages

Most marriages do not collapse from one explosive moment. They erode through quiet, accumulated disappointments that go unnamed, unresolved, and eventually unspoken. Long before couples stop loving each other, they often stop seeing each other. And when someone feels unseen long enough, resentment begins to form its government inside the heart.

Resentment rarely announces itself loudly at first. It whispers. It catalogs. It remembers. It keeps mental records of unmet expectations, unacknowledged sacrifices, and unreturned affection. Over time, those silent records begin shaping perception. What was once grace becomes irritation. What was once patience becomes fatigue. What was once compassion becomes contempt.

Appreciation and resentment cannot occupy the same space for long. One will eventually rule.

Why Men Collapse Without Appreciation

Many men do not require constant affirmation, but they do require recognition. When effort feels invisible, motivation begins to drain. When contribution is assumed instead of acknowledged, initiative weakens. When sacrifice feels expected instead of valued, joy fades from responsibility.

A man who feels appreciated does not merely feel encouraged, he feels anchored. He feels seen in his labor. He feels respected in his burden. He feels understood in his striving. Appreciation becomes the oxygen that keeps his sense of purpose alive inside the home.

Without appreciation, many men do not become louder, they become quieter. They retreat emotionally. They disengage mentally. They numb internally. It is not always rebellion. Often, it is weariness turning inward.

Why Women Are Devastated Without Emotional Safety

While men often collapse without appreciation, many women collapse without emotional safety. When a woman does not feel safe to express pain, doubt, fear, or vulnerability without being dismissed, corrected, mocked, minimized, or punished, her heart instinctively closes.

She may still function.
She may still serve.
She may still manage the household.

But she stops trusting with her tenderness.

And once tenderness withdraws, affection often follows. Intimacy begins to feel dangerous instead of nourishing. Communication becomes guarded instead of shared. The woman is still present, but her heart increasingly lives in self-protection.

How Misunderstanding Turns Into Resentment

Resentment rarely begins with hatred. It begins with misinterpretation. A man feels unappreciated and assumes his wife does not value him. A woman feels emotionally unsafe and assumes her husband does not care about her heart. Each one interprets pain through fear instead of through empathy.

And fear always tells a story that exaggerates threat.

He tells himself, "Nothing I do is ever enough."
She tells herself, "What I feel never matters."

Once those inner narratives take root, interactions are filtered through suspicion instead of trust. Tone is misread. Silence is misinterpreted. Influence is resisted. And gradually, each spouse becomes more focused on self-protection than on mutual understanding.

When Effort Feels Exploited and Vulnerability Feels Punished

At the core of resentment are two devastating internal conclusions:

For many men:
"I give everything, and it still isn't enough."

For many women:
"I open my heart, and it still isn't safe."

When effort feels exploited, generosity dies.
When vulnerability feels punished, intimacy dies.

And when generosity and intimacy die together, marriage becomes mechanical instead of relational.

The Subtle Role of Entitlement

Resentment grows fastest where entitlement is present. Entitlement says, "You owe me without choice." It turns love into obligation and sacrifice into debt. It strips gratitude from relationship and replaces it with demand.

Entitlement rarely begins maliciously. It often grows slowly through unmet expectations that were never renegotiated. Over time, one spouse begins to feel owed for their endurance. The other begins to feel controlled by the weight of invisible rules.

And once entitlement takes root, appreciation cannot survive.

How Resentment Corrupts Memory

One of the most destructive traits of resentment is how it rewrites history. It does not merely respond to the present, it reinterprets the past. What once felt generous now feels calculated. What once felt sacrificial now feels selfish. What once felt loving now feels manipulative.

Resentment does not only distort what is happening. It distorts what has already happened. And when memory is corrupted, hope becomes difficult to sustain, because the past no longer feels trustworthy.

The Moment Appreciation Feels Dangerous

Some spouses resist appreciation not because they are ungrateful, but because gratitude feels like surrender. To thank someone feels like acknowledging dependence. To honor someone feels like relinquishing leverage. To affirm someone feels like losing the ability to withhold.

So appreciation becomes strategic instead of sincere. It is offered sparingly, carefully, even reluctantly. And the very nourishment the relationship needs most becomes rationed.

Where appreciation is withheld as power, resentment thrives as poison.

Why Couples Argue About Surface Issues Instead of the Real Wounds

Many couples argue about money, sex, parenting, schedules, tone, habits, and routines, but the real war is often beneath all of it. The deeper battle is rarely about logistics. It is about wounded value.

He is fighting to feel valued.
She is fighting to feel safe.

Until those two needs are addressed with intention, every surface issue becomes a proxy war for the real injury.

How Honor Starves Resentment

Honor is not flattery. It is the discipline of seeing worth even when wounded. It is the refusal to let disappointment erase dignity. It is the decision to continue valuing someone even while you are still healing from what they have done. Honor does not pretend pain does not exist; it simply refuses to allow pain to redefine a person's identity. It separates behavior from worth without excusing the behavior.

Where honor is restored, appreciation can begin to breathe again. Safety can return again. Respect can grow again. And as honor slowly takes its rightful place, resentment begins to starve, not through confrontation alone, but through the quiet, daily choice to see value where pain once dominated the lens of perception.

The Courage to Appreciate Again After Being Hurt

Appreciation always carries risk in wounded relationships. To affirm again means to reopen vulnerability. To thank again means trusting that giving will not be exploited. To honor again means believing the other person will not misuse the ground you are offering.

This is why appreciation after pain is not shallow, it is brave.

It does not mean all wounds are healed.
It means the heart is choosing not to be governed by fear.

The Only Way Out of the War

There is no shortcut out of resentment. The only exit is mutual confession and mutual courage. One must be willing to admit, "I stopped appreciating you." The other must be willing to admit, "I stopped being safe for you."

Both must be willing to say:
"We both withdrew something essential, and we both want it restored."

Restoration rarely begins when one person becomes perfect.
It begins when both become honest.

When Appreciation and Safety Return Together

When a man begins to feel genuinely appreciated again, his posture changes. His presence strengthens. His motivation resurfaces. His initiative awakens.

They Shall Be One

When a woman begins to feel genuinely safe again, her heart softens. Her communication deepens. Her affection returns. Her vulnerability revives.

When appreciation and safety return together, the marriage often experiences something many thought was gone forever, not youth, not idealism, not fantasy, but tenderness.

And tenderness is what resentment can never tolerate.

CHAPTER 18

WHEN MONEY BECOMES THE ENEMY INSTEAD OF THE ASSIGNMENT

The Illusion of Financial Problems

One of the most common sentences spoken in struggling marriages is, "We have money problems." But in pastoral reality, most couples do not actually have money problems. They have partnership problems that money has exposed. Finances are rarely the root. They are the revealer.

Money has a way of unmasking fear, control, insecurity, distrust, misalignment, and hidden power struggles. It exposes whether a couple sees themselves as a team facing a common assignment, or as individuals defending separate territories.

When money becomes the enemy, it is usually because the couple stopped standing on the same side of the issue.

How Fear Turns Spouses Into Adversaries

Financial pressure has a unique way of awakening survival instincts. When fear rises, people instinctively shift into self-protection. Instead of thinking, "How do we face this together?" they begin thinking, often without realizing it, "How do I secure myself?" That subtle shift in posture is powerful enough to transform partners into opponents without either person ever intending for that to happen.

Over time, unspoken roles begin to form. One spouse becomes the risk-taker, the other the gatekeeper. One becomes the spender, the other the withholder. One begins to feel controlled, while the other feels burdened by responsibility. Neither role is chosen with malice, yet both are shaped by fear. And slowly, almost imperceptibly, the battlefield becomes the bank account, not because money is evil, but because survival has replaced partnership.

When Provision Is Reduced to Control

In some homes, the one who earns becomes the one who governs. Money quietly becomes a tool of leverage rather than a stewarded resource. Decisions are made unilaterally. Discussion becomes permission-seeking. And partnership dissolves into hierarchy driven by income instead of covenant.

True provision does not dominate, it covers.

When provision becomes control, the marriage stops feeling like collaboration and starts feeling like supervision.

When Independence Masquerades as Wisdom

At the opposite extreme are couples who refuse to unify financially altogether. Separate accounts. Separate goals. Separate strategies. Separate sacrifices. The language of independence often sounds responsible, but it frequently hides a deeper fear of vulnerability.

Financial unity requires exposure.
It requires trust.
It requires accountability.
It requires shared risk.

Independence often feels safer because it limits emotional and financial intimacy. Yet marriages built on financial isolation rarely experience true economic peace, because peace was never designed to exist without mutual stewardship.

Why Money Magnifies Spiritual Posture

Money itself is neutral. It simply magnifies what already governs a heart. Where fear rules, money becomes a source of anxiety. Where pride rules, money becomes a marker of worth. Where greed rules, money becomes an appetite. Where control rules, money becomes leverage.

But where God rules, money becomes an assignment under stewardship.

Scripture never treats money as merely personal provision. It consistently frames it as a stewardship connected to purpose, generosity, obedience, and trust.

When Couples Stop Talking and Start Tracking

One of the most dangerous shifts in financial tension is when conversation disappears and silent tracking begins. One spouse starts watching purchases instead of discussing priorities. The other starts hiding expenses instead of sharing struggles.

Transparency gives way to surveillance.
Trust gives way to accounting.
Unity gives way to suspicion.

Once secrecy enters finances, intimacy rarely remains far behind.

Why Debt Feels Moral Even When It's Structural

Debt carries enormous emotional weight in marriage. It often feels like failure, shame, irresponsibility, or betrayal, even when the debt itself is structural rather than reckless. Cultural pressure teaches people that debt is not just financial, it is moral.

This moralization of money often causes couples to speak with contempt rather than compassion. They stop addressing systems and start attacking character. One becomes the "irresponsible one." The other becomes the "rigid one." Labels replace language. And shame replaces strategy.

The Power of Seeing Money as "Our Assignment"

The turning point for many couples is the moment they stop saying, "Your spending" and "My income," and start saying, "Our assignment."

When money becomes an assignment:
Fear becomes strategy.
Blame becomes planning.
Conflict becomes budgeting.
Pressure becomes problem-solving.

Assignment language removes personal attack and restores shared responsibility.

When One Carries the Financial Weight Alone

In many marriages, one spouse carries the mental load of finances entirely. They track every bill. They remember every deadline. They feel every pressure. The other remains loosely aware but emotionally detached. Over time, this imbalance creates exhaustion on one side and ignorance on the other.

The one who carries the weight grows resentful.
The one who avoids the weight grows defensive.

Money becomes lonely work when it was designed to be shared stewardship.

Why Money Exposes Honor Faster Than Almost Anything Else

How a couple speaks about money often reveals how they truly honor one another. Do they consult or decide? Do they invite or inform? Do they plan or impose? Do they listen or override?

Honor says, "I will not treat your voice as optional simply because I earn more."

Honor says, "I will not treat provision as permission to govern alone."

Where honor reigns, money becomes a tool of blessing.
Where honor is absent, money becomes a weapon of division.

When God Is Asked to Bless a Budget He Was Never Invited to Lead

Many couples ask God to bless their finances after decisions have already been made. They pray after debt is accumulated. They intercede after impulsive spending. They seek relief after unaligned priorities. But God was never invited into the strategy, only into the crisis.

Healing begins when couples say, "Lord, You are not just our rescuer, you are our Director."

Provision flows most freely where God governs the plan, not merely patches the fallout.

From Financial Tension to Financial Teamwork

When couples truly return to partnership, money begins to lose its power to divide. Conversations open again. Planning becomes shared again. Dreams begin to surface again. Adjustments are made together again. Sacrifice becomes mutual again. The numbers on the page may not change immediately, but the alignment always does. And alignment has a way of inviting provision in ways fear never can. Where unity is restored, peace returns first, and provision often follows.

The question that restores peace in financial conflict is not, "Who is right?" The question that heals is, "Are we standing on the same side again?" Because the moment partners become teammates instead of opponents, money loses its authority to dominate the marriage. It returns to its proper place, as a tool, not a tyrant.

CHAPTER 19

FROM LOVERS TO STRANGERS: HOW FRIENDSHIP DIES IN MARRIAGE, AND HOW IT CAN LIVE AGAIN

When the Marriage Still Works, But the Relationship Feels Gone

There are marriages that function flawlessly on the outside and yet feel emotionally barren on the inside. The bills are paid. The children are raised. The routines continue. The home appears stable. But somewhere along the way, friendship quietly slipped out the back door. Without a dramatic moment, without a defining collapse, connection simply thinned until it became distant.

They no longer talk about dreams the way they once did. They no longer laugh with ease. They no longer share thoughts freely. They no longer enjoy each other's presence without an agenda attached. They are no longer enemies, but neither are they companions. They have become strangers who share a life.

This kind of distance is often harder to diagnose than open conflict because it hides behind civility. Nothing is obviously broken, yet nothing feels alive either. The marriage is not violent, it is vacant. And that quiet vacancy can be just as destructive as loud division, because it slowly starves the soul while everything appears "fine."

How Responsibility Slowly Replaces Relationship

One of the great thieves of marital friendship is responsibility without romance. Life becomes heavy. Children require attention.

Careers demand energy. Crises interrupt rest. And slowly, the relationship becomes a system of logistics instead of a space of delight.

Conversation turns into scheduling.
Touch turns into necessity.
Time turns into obligation.

The marriage becomes efficient but no longer intimate.

When Communication Becomes Transactional

Many couples still speak often but rarely connect. Their words are functional rather than personal. They exchange information instead of hearts. They update each other rather than invite each other.

"How was your day?" becomes a formality instead of an inquiry.
"I'm tired" becomes a statement instead of an invitation.
"I love you" becomes habitual instead of intentional.

Transactional communication keeps life moving, but it rarely keeps love growing.

Why Friendship Dies Before Passion Does

Sex can survive after friendship dies, for a season. Romance can function mechanically. But intimacy eventually starves without relational warmth. Bodies may connect long after hearts have drifted, but passion eventually becomes effort instead of overflow.

Friendship is what makes desire safe. It makes affection nourishing instead of performative. It makes intimacy feel mutual rather than demanded.

Without friendship, passion increasingly feels empty.

The Unspoken Grief of Becoming Unknown Again

One of the deepest griefs a person can feel in marriage is not betrayal, it is becoming unknown by the one who once knew them best. They still share a bed, but not an inner world. They still share space, but not thoughts. They still share history, but not hope.

This kind of grief is quiet. And because it is quiet, it often goes untreated.

Why People Stop Being Curious About Each Other

At the beginning of love, curiosity is effortless. Every detail feels important. Every thought feels worth hearing. But as familiarity increases, curiosity often decreases. We assume we already know the person. We stop asking. We stop listening. We stop exploring who they are becoming.

And yet, people are not static.
They evolve.
They mature.
They change.

When curiosity dies, we keep relating to an old version of our spouse while they quietly become someone new.

The Silent Role of Discouragement

Many stop investing emotionally not because they no longer care, but because they are tired of trying and not being met. After enough unanswered bids for connection, the heart learns to conserve energy. It stops reaching. It stops hoping. It stops risking.

Distance is often not rejection.
It is self-protection after repeated disappointment.

Rebuilding Friendship Is Not Romantic, It Is Relational

Friendship rarely returns through grand gestures. It returns through small, consistent, humble reconnections. Through unscheduled conversations. Through shared laughter. Through curiosity without agenda. Through presence without performance.

Friendship is not rebuilt through intensity.
It is rebuilt through attention.

Learning to Talk Again Without Defensiveness

One of the most powerful steps toward restored friendship is learning to speak without armor. Not to convince. Not to correct. Not to control. But simply to be known again.

This requires listening without preparing rebuttal.
It requires responding without dismissing.
It requires curiosity without assumption.

Friendship cannot survive where defensiveness rules.

When Laughter Returns, So Does Hope

One of the earliest signs that friendship is returning is laughter. Not forced humor. Not polite smiles. But spontaneous joy. Shared amusement. Common delight.

Laughter is often the sound of safety returning.

From Coexistence Back to Companionship

Marriage was never meant to be a durable institution alone. It was meant to be a living companionship. Not just two people sharing responsibility, but two souls enjoying partnership.

Restoring friendship does not erase history.
But it restores the possibility of future joy.

The Question That Revives Friendship

The question that often begins the journey back to companionship is simple, and brave:

"Do you still want to be my friend again?"

Not as a formality.
But as an invitation.

And where that invitation is accepted, even slowly, life begins to breathe again in the marriage.

CHAPTER 20
WHAT MEN NEED TO KNOW ABOUT WOMEN

Why Fixing Feels Loving, but Often Misses the Moment

Men are instinctive fixers. It is in their design to identify problems, assess threats, and bring resolution. This instinct is not sinful, it is wired into masculinity as a form of protection and provision. A man feels valuable when he can solve. He feels effective when he can repair. He feels purposeful when he can bring order to chaos.

But what many men do not realize is that a woman is often not communicating in order to be fixed. She is communicating in order to be heard, known, and emotionally joined. When a man immediately reaches for a solution, he may believe he is being loving, yet what she often experiences instead is emotional bypassing.

To her, it can feel like:
"You didn't sit with me."
"You didn't enter my world."
"You skipped past my heart to get to your answer."

And the very instinct meant to help ends up unintentionally creating distance.

Why Hearing Is Often More Intimate Than Solving

For many women, emotional safety is built through attunement, not resolution. She feels bonded not when a problem is eliminated, but when a person remains present inside the tension. Presence communicates value. Attention communicates worth. Listening communicates dignity.

When a man slows down enough to listen without interrupting, correcting, minimizing, or diagnosing, he is offering something far more powerful than a solution, he is offering emotional shelter.

Being heard says:
"You matter."
"Your inner world matters."
"Your perspective matters."
"You do not have to rush out of your feelings to be lovable."

In that moment, she is not looking for the problem to disappear. She is looking to not be alone inside it.

Why Immediate Solutions Can Feel Dismissive

When a man immediately offers a fix, a woman can interpret it, often unconsciously, as:
"This is simple."
"This shouldn't be upsetting you."
"There's no need to feel this way if you just do this."

Even if that was never the man's intent, the effect can still be one of emotional reduction. Her experience feels minimized. Her process feels rushed. Her complexity feels flattened.

Men often hear:
"There is a problem. I must resolve it."

Women are often saying:
"There is a feeling. Will you enter it with me?"

Those are not the same requests.

The Flower in the Parking Lot

This is why the flower example matters so deeply.

If a man is driving with his wife and passes a man selling flowers in a parking lot and the woman says, "Aren't those flowers beautiful?", the man who immediately pulls into the lot and buys them believes he is being romantic.

But what she often experiences instead is:
"You acted because I prompted you."
"You didn't remember."
"You reacted, you didn't initiate."

Far more meaningful to her is when a week or two later, unprompted, he walks in the door with those same flowers. Why? Because now the flowers carry memory, not impulse. They carry attention, not pressure. They represent:

"You listened."
"You remembered."
"You valued what mattered to me enough to carry it with you."

To a woman, remembered words feel like love stored and returned. To a man, immediate action feels like love expressed.

This is not right versus wrong.
It is difference in emotional language.

Why Women Talk Through Feelings Instead of Past Them

Many women process emotionally out loud. For them, talking is not merely communication, it is integration. As she speaks, she is not just sharing information; she is making sense of her inner world in real time. Words help organize what she feels. Language becomes the pathway through which emotion is understood, sorted, and eventually calmed.

This is why interruptions can feel invasive. Corrections can feel dismissive. And solutions can feel premature. She is not finished feeling yet, and she does not want to be rushed past the feeling in order to arrive at a fix. The expression itself is part of the healing. The articulation is part of the clarity. To be heard is not a step toward resolution—it is the first form of resolution.

For many men, silence often means thought. For many women, speech often means thought. Neither is wrong. They are simply different languages of processing. And when a husband learns to honor this difference rather than correct it, listening itself becomes one of the most powerful ways he can love.

When Men Feel Overwhelmed by Emotion

Many men feel overwhelmed by emotional intensity, not because they lack love, but because emotion does not feel structured to them. Feelings feel fluid, vague, layered, and unresolved. Men prefer clarity. Women often communicate through complexity.

So when a woman is speaking emotionally, a man can feel:
"I don't know what to do with this."
"I don't know what's being asked of me."
"I need to fix this so it will stop."

But what she may be asking is not for the storm to stop, she may be asking him to stay inside it with her.

The Difference Between Support and Solving

Solving and support may sound similar, but they speak two very different emotional languages. Solving says, "Here is the answer." Support says, "I am here with you while you feel." Solving brings an ending to a problem; support strengthens the bond between two people while the problem is still being processed. Solving brings a sense of control; support builds trust. One is task-oriented. The other is connection-oriented. Both have their place, but confusing one for the other can quietly wound a relationship.

A woman does not ultimately feel secure because problems are rare. She feels secure because presence is predictable. Safety is not built on the absence of difficulty, but on the consistent assurance that she will not be emotionally abandoned inside the difficulty. When she knows her husband will remain present without rushing her, fixing her, or correcting her feelings, security deepens. In that environment, trust grows naturally, and trust is the soil where intimacy truly flourishes.

Why Women Stop Talking When They Are Always Fixed

Many women eventually stop sharing emotionally not because the pain disappeared, but because the response trained them to retreat. After enough interruptions, diagnoses, corrections, and solutions, her heart quietly concludes: "It is safer to keep this inside."

And when women stop talking, men often assume peace has arrived, when in reality, distance has. Silence does not mean resolution. Often, it means withdrawal of trust.

What Women Need More Than Answers

More than answers, women long to be chosen in the moment, prioritized in the exchange, and held emotionally before they are handled practically. They want to be felt before they are figured out. This does not mean that men should never offer solutions. It simply means that timing and permission matter more than efficiency. When solutions arrive too quickly, they can feel like erasure rather than care.

One simple question has the power to change everything: "Do you want me to fix this, or just listen right now?" That single moment of consent restores dignity, honors emotion, and reestablishes safety in seconds. It tells her, "Your heart matters more than my answer." And when that message is received, walls fall, trust rises, and connection is reactivated almost instantly.

Why Remembering Speaks Louder Than Reacting

To remember something a woman said days or weeks earlier and act on it later communicates:
"You stayed with me after the moment passed."
"I carried your words with me."
"You did not treat my thoughts as temporary."

Memory is one of the most underestimated forms of love.

It tells her:
"You live in me even when you're not present."

The Invitation to Men

What many men must unlearn is not strength, but speed. The speed to resolve. The speed to correct. The speed to stabilize. Love sometimes moves slower than instinct.

And what many men must learn is not passivity, but presence.

Presence that listens without rescuing.

Presence that stays without fixing.
Presence that holds without controlling.
Presence that remembers without being told.

This kind of presence does not make a man weak.
It makes him trusted.

The Question Every Man Must Ask

Instead of asking,
"How do I solve this?"

The deeper question is:
"How do I make her feel safe to keep letting me into her inner world?"

Because when safety stays alive, communication never has to disappear.

CHAPTER 21
WHAT WOMEN NEED TO KNOW ABOUT MEN

A Man's Greatest Fear Is Not Failure, It Is Being Misunderstood

Most men do not fear failing as much as they fear being misjudged. Failure can be corrected. Skills can be learned. Strategies can be adjusted. But to be misunderstood, especially by the woman whose opinion matters most, cuts much deeper.

A man longs to be seen accurately. More than praise, he wants his intentions to be understood. He wants his efforts to be interpreted correctly. He wants his heart to be recognized even when his execution is imperfect. Many men are not crushed by correction itself, they are crushed by misinterpretation. When what they meant in love is received as indifference, when what they tried in good faith is judged only by what fell short, discouragement quietly sets in.

But when a man feels truly seen, when his motive is acknowledged even as his methods are refined, strength rises again. Understanding does for a man what safety does for a woman: it restores confidence, steadies the soul, and draws him back into connection instead of retreat.

When a man feels constantly misunderstood, he does not become louder, he becomes guarded. He begins to explain less. Try less. Share less. Risk less. His silence is not usually apathy. It is often the language of resignation.

Why Appreciation Does More Than Compliment Ever Could

Many women express love through care, closeness, and communication. Many men experience love most deeply through appreciation. Appreciation is not praise for ego, it is recognition for effort. It tells a man, "You matter here. What you carry matters here. What you do is seen here."

A man who feels appreciated does not simply feel encouraged, he feels anchored. He feels emotionally rooted in the marriage. He feels connected to the purpose of the home. He feels necessary in a way that fortifies his identity.

Without appreciation, many men begin to feel invisible. And when invisibility settles in, motivation quietly drains away.

Why Correction Often Feels Like Contempt

Correction and criticism do not land the same in a man's heart as they do in a woman's. Many women can hear correction and still feel loved. Many men, however, hear repeated correction as a signal of disapproval, not improvement.

To a man's inner world, constant correction often translates to:
"I am failing."
"I am not enough."
"I disappoint you."
"I do not measure up."

Even when a woman's intent is growth, a man may experience it as contempt. This does not mean women should never speak truth, but it means tone, timing, and affirmation must surround truth, or it will be interpreted as rejection.

Why Men Withdraw Instead of Exploding

When men feel disrespected, misunderstood, or unappreciated, many do not argue, they withdraw. Silence becomes a shelter. Distance becomes defense. Work becomes refuge. Distraction becomes escape.

This is often misread as indifference.
In reality, it is often shame.

A man who believes he is failing often goes quiet, not because he doesn't care, but because he does not know how to stay present without feeling exposed.

Silence Is Often the Sound of Overwhelm, Not Absence of Love

Many women experience silence as abandonment. Many men experience silence as self-regulation. They go quiet not to punish, but to stabilize. Emotion can feel disorganizing to a man's internal world. Silence gives him ordering space.

The tragedy occurs when:
She interprets silence as disinterest.
He experiences silence as necessary survival.

Two different emotional languages collide without translation.

Why Men Protect Through Provision

Many men instinctively demonstrate love through provision and protection. They work longer. They press harder. They take responsibility seriously. They shoulder invisible burdens. They internalize pressure.

And yet, when their efforts are reduced to "you're never home" or "you only care about work," many men feel emotionally erased. What they intended as provision feels interpreted as neglect.

This creates a painful gap between intent and interpretation.

What Many Women Don't See: The Weight Men Carry Quietly

Many men walk through life carrying:
The fear of not being enough.
The pressure of responsibility.
The weight of financial expectations.
The stress of leadership.
The anxiety of failure.

But they rarely speak it, because they were never trained that vulnerability would be received with safety. Many were taught that exposure costs respect.

So they carry silently.
And silence makes the weight heavier.

Why Men Need to Be Understood, Not Just Corrected

A man does not only want to be told what is wrong.
He deeply longs to be told:
"I see why this is hard for you."
"I understand what you're carrying."
"I know you don't always know how to express this."
"I don't think you're failing, you're trying."

Understanding does not excuse wrongdoing.
But it opens the door for change without shame.

Shame shuts men down.
Understanding draws men out.

The Power of Speaking to a Man's Intention, Not Just His Outcome

Many men live with the quiet pain of knowing their heart is good, but their execution is flawed. When only outcomes are addressed and intentions go unseen, they begin to feel fundamentally misjudged.

When a woman says,
"I know you didn't mean to hurt me,"
something in a man's soul exhales.

When she says,
"I know you were trying in your own way,"
his heart reopens.

Intent does not erase impact.
But recognizing intent restores relational dignity.

Why Men Crave Respect More Than They Can Articulate

Respect affirms a man's position, identity, and value. It reassures him that he is trusted, not just tolerated. That he is admired, not merely assessed. That he is a partner, not a project.

Without respect, many men feel disqualified in their own home.

And when a man feels disqualified:
He either becomes passive…
Or he becomes defensive.

Neither posture brings peace.

When a Man Feels Safe, He Softens

One of the great misunderstandings in marriage is the belief that safety only softens women. It softens men as well. When a man feels understood, respected, appreciated, and trusted, his wall begins to lower. His tenderness returns. His vulnerability awakens. His listening deepens. The hardness so many women encounter in men is rarely natural, it is most often learned protection. It is the outer shell built from years of misinterpretation, pressure, failure, and unprocessed disappointment. When safety is restored, that shell no longer needs to remain.

This is where the invitation to women must be rightly understood. The call is not to carry men, to fix men, or to mother men. It is to see them clearly. To understand without emasculating. To respect without disappearing. To affirm without flattering. To challenge without contempt. These are deeply spiritual skills, rooted not in control but in honor. A man does not need perfection from his wife. He needs partnership that believes in him while he is in the process of becoming.

The Question Every Woman Must Ask

Instead of asking,
"Why won't he open up?"

The deeper question is:
"Has he felt safe enough to be truly seen?"

Because when a man feels understood, not managed, he does not hide.

He shows up.

CHAPTER 22

A NEW BEGINNING: A STEP-BY-STEP PATH TO HEALING AND HARMONY

You have seen the principles.
You have faced the pain.
You have recognized the patterns.

Now you need a path.

This chapter is not theory. It is a manual. If you will walk through these steps, slowly, honestly, and consistently, you will set your marriage on a new path toward healing, harmony, and partnership.

You cannot change the past.
But you can absolutely surrender the present and redirect the future.

Let's walk this out, line upon line.

STEP 1 – Return to the Beginning With God

What to do:
Set aside a specific time, no phones, no television, no distractions, and together acknowledge before God how your marriage began.

How to do it:
1. Sit together, facing each other.
2. One of you pray out loud something like:
   "Lord, we acknowledge that in many ways we began this marriage without fully seeking You. Today, we invite You into our covenant as Lord and Architect. We repent for

leading ourselves and ask You to lead us from this point forward."
3. Take turns briefly confessing (without blaming each other) where you know you made decisions without God's wisdom:
   - "I rushed…"
   - "I ignored warning signs…"
   - "I made assumptions…"
4. End by holding hands and saying together, out loud: "From this day forward, this is Your marriage. We surrender it to You."

Why this matters:
Healing must start at the origin point. You are not erasing your history; you are relocating your Lordship.

STEP 2 – Own Your Part Without Defending Yourself

What to do:
Each spouse takes responsibility for their contribution to the pain, without explanation, justification, or counter-accusation.

How to do it:
1. Choose who will share first. The other listens without interrupting.
2. Speak in "I" statements, not "you" statements:
   - "I shut down when you needed me to listen."
   - "I used anger to control the room."
   - "I withheld affection."
   - "I let resentment build instead of speaking earlier."
3. Do not balance the scale by responding with, "Yes, but you…"
4. After each confession, the other spouse responds with only:

- "Thank you for owning that," or
- "I receive that, and I forgive you." (even if your emotions are catching up slowly)

Why this matters:
You cannot heal what you keep defending. Repentance is not self-condemnation. It is opening the door for God to work.

STEP 3 – Establish One Non-Negotiable Prayer Rhythm

What to do:
Choose one simple, sustainable rhythm of praying together, and commit to it as if your marriage depends on it, because it does.

How to do it:
1. Decide on a time you can actually keep:
   - Before bed
   - Right after dinner
   - In the car before work

2. Keep the prayer short and sincere, not long and pressured:
   - "Lord, we give You this day and this marriage. Heal where we've hurt each other. Teach us how to love like You love us. Amen."

3. Hold hands while praying, touch matters.
4. If one spouse is less comfortable praying out loud, let the other carry the verbal load at first. The quieter one can simply add, "Lord, I agree," or, "Help us."

Why this matters:
Praying together is not about eloquence or length. It is about agreement and humility. It shifts the atmosphere and reminds both of you: We are not the only ones in this marriage. Christ is here.

STEP 4 – Rebuild Safety Through One Honest Conversation at a Time

What to do:
Begin a weekly "Safe Conversation" time where the goal is not fixing, defending, or debating, but understanding.

How to do it:
1. Set a weekly time: 30–60 minutes.
2. Agree to these rules before you begin:
   - No raising voices.
   - No interrupting.
   - No name-calling or sarcasm.
   - No threats of leaving.

3. Use this simple structure:
   - One spouse shares:
     "This is how I've been feeling lately…"
   - The other responds:
     "What I hear you saying is…"
   - Then ask:
     "Did I understand you correctly?"

4. Only after the first person feels "fully heard" can any solution or response be offered.
5. Switch roles.

Why this matters:
Safety is rebuilt every time a person risks honesty and is not punished for it. You are training your nervous systems to see each other as safe again.

STEP 5 – Learn the "Listen Before You Fix" Principle

What to do:
Especially for husbands, practice listening without jumping to solutions. For wives, practice stating what you need in the moment.

How to do it:
1. When your spouse begins to share a struggle, ask:
   - "Do you want me to just listen, or do you want my help fixing this?"

2. If they say "Just listen," then:
   - Maintain eye contact.
   - Ask clarifying questions:
     "How did that make you feel?"
     "What hurt the most about that?"
   - Resist the urge to solve. Your job in that moment is to stay present.

3. If they say, "I'd like your help," then offer your thoughts gently, not as commands.

Why this matters:
Many spouses are not asking for a mechanic. They are asking for a witness. Listening is often more healing than the most efficient fix.

STEP 6 – Restore Honor With Daily Words of Value

What to do:
Begin reintroducing honor and appreciation on purpose, even when you don't feel it fully yet.

How to do it:
1. Commit to one statement of appreciation per day toward your spouse.

Examples:
- "Thank you for working so hard for our family."
- "I appreciate how you handled the kids today."
- "I noticed you were patient when I wasn't."

2. Do not mix appreciation with a complaint:
   - Not: "Thanks for finally doing the dishes."
   - But: "Thank you for doing the dishes tonight."

3. Once a week, speak a bigger affirmation:
   - "Here's something I admire about who you are..."

Why this matters:
Resentment starves where honor is restored. You are choosing to see again what disappointment made you blind to.

STEP 7 – Make Money a Shared Assignment, Not a Silent War

What to do:
Take finances out of the shadows and bring them into shared partnership.

How to do it:
1. Schedule a calm "Money Meeting" (not in the middle of a fight).
2. Begin with this statement out loud:
   - "Our enemy is not each other. Our enemy is confusion, fear, and lack. We are on the same team."
3. Put the numbers on the table—no hiding, no shaming. Just data.
4. Ask together:
   - "What is our current reality?"

- "What do we need to adjust?"
- "What can we agree on as a first step?"

5. Pray briefly:

"Lord, this is Your money. Give us wisdom and unity as we steward it."

Why this matters:
Money becomes a weapon when it is ruled by fear and secrecy. Healing comes when it becomes a shared assignment under God.

STEP 8 – Rebuild Friendship With Small, Predictable Moments

What to do:
Instead of waiting for big vacations or perfect date nights, deliberately reintroduce small, consistent joys that rebuild friendship.

How to do it:
1. Choose one weekly friendship rhythm:
   - A walk together
   - Coffee on the porch
   - A drive with no agenda
   - Watching a show you both enjoy

2. Use this time not to rehash problems, but to:
   - Laugh
   - Reminisce
   - Dream
   - Share light-hearted thoughts

3. Re-learn to ask curious questions:

- "What's been on your mind lately?"
- "If you could change one thing about our routines, what would it be?"
- "What's something you're looking forward to?"

Why this matters:
Lovers cannot stay connected if friends have disappeared. Friendship is the soil that romance grows from.

STEP 9 – Rekindle Affection Without Pressure

What to do:
Rebuild physical connection gently, respectfully, and gradually, without demanding intimacy as proof of progress.

How to do it:
1. Start with non-sexual affection:
   - Holding hands
   - A hug that lingers a little longer
   - A hand on the shoulder or back

2. Communicate:
   - "I just want to be close to you—no pressure, no expectation."

3. Make room for honest conversation about intimacy when the time is right:
   - Fears
   - Wounds
   - Misunderstandings

4. Decide together to move at a pace that honors both hearts.

Why this matters:
Bodies cannot trust where hearts still feel unsafe. Affection is a bridge, not a demand.

STEP 10 – Commit to Becoming, Not Just Repairing

What to do:
Decide that this is not just about "fixing what's broken," but about becoming who God intended as husband and wife.

How to do it:
1. Each spouse privately asks:
    - "Lord, what kind of husband/wife are You calling me to become?"

2. Write down what comes to your heart:
    - "More patient…"
    - "More present…"
    - "More courageous…"
    - "More gentle…"

3. Share one or two of these with each other—not as demands, but as personal commitments:
    - "I want to grow in listening."
    - "I want to stop shutting down when I'm hurt."

4. Revisit this conversation every few months and update where you see growth.

Why this matters:
Marriage is not simply the repair of two damaged histories. It is the formation of two living testimonies.

STEP 11 – Decide Together: We Will Not War Against Each Other

What to do:
Make a covenant, in God's presence, that you will no longer be each other's enemy.

How to do it:
1. Stand together, hold hands, and look each other in the eyes.
2. Say something like this, out loud, together:
   "We are not each other's enemy.
   We refuse to fight as opponents.
   From this day forward, we will fight for our covenant, not against each other.

   When we fail, we will repent.
   When we hurt, we will speak.
   When we struggle, we will seek God.
   We choose partnership over pride, process over pretending, and growth over giving up.
   In Jesus' Name, amen."

Why this matters:
Lines must be drawn. At some point, you stop negotiating with destruction and you stand together against it.

STEP 12 – Give Your Marriage Permission to Become New

Finally, remember this:
You are not trying to get back to how it once was.
You are inviting God to make it what it has never been yet.

Give yourselves permission:
- To grow slowly

They Shall Be One

- To celebrate small shifts
- To try again after setbacks
- To believe that God is not finished with you

You have confronted your patterns. You have heard the truth about man and woman, head and helper, love and covenant. This chapter is your how-to path.

If you will walk it, not perfectly, but consistently you will not simply have a marriage that survived. You can have a marriage that has been rebuilt on purpose, partnership, and presence.

And truly…

They shall be one.

CONCLUSION
THE RETURN TO ONE

Marriage was never meant to be endured, it was meant to be built. It was never meant to be managed, it was meant to be stewarded. And it was never meant to be survived, it was meant to be multiplied into legacy.

If you have read this far, it means you are no longer pretending that proximity alone produces unity. You now understand that intimacy must be cultivated, safety must be restored, covenant must be chosen daily, and purpose must be shared intentionally. You now know that conflict is not the enemy, fear is. Difference is not the threat, misinterpretation is. Growth is not betrayal, insecurity is.

You now know that romance alone cannot sustain what only covenant can carry. You now know that submission without trust is distortion, leadership without sacrifice is domination, and love without honor is fragile. And perhaps most importantly, you now know this: marriage can be healed, not by trying harder, but by returning deeper.

Returning to design.
Returning to safety.
Returning to God.
Returning to one.

Healing does not mean perfection. Harmony does not mean the absence of conflict. Oneness does not mean the loss of identity. It means alignment. It means rhythm. It means two lives learning how to move again with one heartbeat.

And if your marriage is still tender…
Still fragile…
Still trying to breathe again…

Know this: God does not heal with accusation. He heals with alignment.

He does not shame what was broken.
He restores what was wounded.

You are not late.
You are not disqualified.
And you are not beyond repair.

The only question that remains is this:

Will you now choose, together, to build?

A FINAL WORD TO HUSBANDS AND WIVES

To the husband: you were never called to dominate, perform, impress, or prove. You were called to cover, love, sacrifice, listen, and lead in Christ. Strength in the Kingdom is always measured by how safely others can rest beneath it.

To the wife: you were never called to disappear, endure silently, or carry what was never yours to hold alone. You were called to fortify mission, multiply vision, protect purpose, and partner in power. Alignment does not erase you, it activates you.

You do not stand on opposite sides of the marriage.
You stand on the same ground, facing the same future.

And that future begins with what you choose next.

A PRAYER FOR COUPLES

Father,

We come to You not as perfect people, but as willing partners.
We lay down pride.
We release fear.
We surrender the need to win.
And we choose again each other.

Where safety was broken, restore it.
Where trust was violated, rebuild it.
Where love grew tired, renew it.
Where hope felt fragile, strengthen it.

We invite You not just into our ceremony, but into our construction.
Not just into our past, but into our future.
Not just into our prayers, but into our decisions.

Teach us how to listen without defense.
Teach us how to speak without wounding.
Teach us how to forgive without keeping score.
Teach us how to grow without competing.

Let our marriage become a sanctuary.
Let our home become an altar.
Let our partnership become a witness of Christ and His Church.

We repent, not in regret, but in alignment.
We return, not in shame, but in trust.
We begin again, not alone, but with You at the center.

In Jesus' name,
Amen.

FOR REFLECTION & REBUILDING

You may wish to reflect on these questions privately or together:
- Where did safety begin to fracture in our marriage?
- What unspoken fears have been shaping our reactions?
- Have we been operating in survival or stewardship?
- Do we still know why we are together?
- What would it look like to truly rebuild as partners again?

There are no right answers, only honest ones.

ABOUT THE AUTHOR

Christopher Turney is a Kingdom teacher, apostolic voice, author, and spiritual father with a passion for restoring sonship, strengthening covenant, and revealing the nature of God the Father to a generation hungry for truth and healing. He is the founder and senior leader of Kingdom Reign Ministries, an apostolic ministry dedicated to establishing Kingdom culture through discipleship, leadership development, and revelatory teaching.

For over two decades, Christopher has walked with individuals, couples, families, and leaders through some of life's most challenging seasons, helping restore identity, rebuild trust, and realign lives with God's original design. His ministry emphasis centers on sonship, honor, covenant, spiritual authority, and the restoration of healthy relationships both in the home and in the Church.

Christopher is known for his ability to blend deep biblical revelation with practical, accessible application. His teaching carries both theological depth and pastoral tenderness, addressing not only what is true, but how that truth heals real lives.

He is the author of several foundational works, including:
- We Wrestle Not: A Kingdom Perspective of Spiritual Warfare
- Called to Sonship
- They Shall Be Saved
- Tithing: Law or Liberty
- The Ekklesia

And now, They Shall Be One, a work born not only from Scripture and revelation, but from years of sitting across tables from wounded couples, walking with families through restoration, and witnessing firsthand what happens when God is invited into the rebuilding of covenant.

Christopher and his wife serve together in ministry and family life, carrying a shared burden to see homes restored, marriages healed, and generations realigned with truth.

CONTACT

Thank you for reading 'They Shall Be One: A Blueprint for Marital Harmony & Healing'. It is my sincere prayer that these pages have strengthened your understanding of covenant, restored hope where discouragement once lived, and given you practical tools for rebuilding safely and intentionally.

If this book has impacted your life, your marriage, or your ministry, and you would like to connect further, invite teaching, or explore counseling, conferences, or training opportunities, you may reach us through the following channels:

Kingdom Reign Ministries
Jensen Beach, Florida
United States

Website:
www.chrisandjillturney.com

Email:
chris@krmchurch.com

You are also welcome to follow Kingdom Reign Ministries on social media for ongoing teachings, marriage resources, leadership training, and Kingdom-focused content.

No matter where you are in your journey, whether rebuilding, strengthening, or learning to trust again, know this: healing is possible, unity is attainable, and covenant is worth building.

www.ingramcontent.com/pod-product-compliance
Lightning Source LLC
Chambersburg PA
CBHW060835190426
43197CB00040B/2612